The Unseen War

The Jezebel Afflicted Soul:
A Quest For Freedom on the Road To Glory and Holiness (Isaiah 35:8)

Alena Moore

REJOICE
Essential Publishing

Alena Moore/Rejoice Essential Publishing

PO BOX 512

Effingham, SC 29541

www.republishing.org

Book Cover: moorecreatives@gmail.com

Unless otherwise indicated, scripture is taken from the King James Version.

The Unseen War/Alena Moore

ISBN-13: 9781956775419

LCCN: 2022917390

Dedication

I dedicate this book to the power of the Holy Spirit, who is teaching me every step of the way on my road to glory. Even though it took me an exceptionally long time to realize and understand what the Holy Spirit was communicating to me, I am forever grateful that He never gave up on me. He kept pursuing me into His presence to heal and live an abundant freedom, glorious knowledge, and wisdom to pass along to my family, friends, the body of Christ, and a lost and dying world.

The Spirit searches out the deep things of God. There is a yearning within every person to connect to their creator. *1 Corinthians 2:9 NIV, "However, as it is written, what no eye has seen, what no ear has heard, and what no human mind has conceived, the things God has prepared for those who love him."* As you allow your spirit to become influenced by the Holy Spirit, you will experience the transforming power that comes only through a relationship with God. The truth of God, Christ Jesus, will affect your emotions, desires, hobbies, and thoughts.

As fear, unforgiveness, hatred, and hopelessness grip society, I want to share how I gained freedom and healing from Satan's demonic attacks through God's transforming power. Through the instruction of the Holy Spirit, I learned to appreciate my identity as a daughter of Christ, and in my obedience, I allowed Him to change me from the inside out. I died to my flesh so the warrior inside could arise in His glory.

Psalms 119:1-5, TPT, "You're only truly happy when you walk in total integrity, walking in the light of God's word. What joy overwhelms everyone who keeps the ways of God, those who seek him as their heart's passion. They'll never do what's wrong. They will always choose the path of the Lord. God has prescribed the right way to live, obeying all his laws with all our hearts. How I long for my life to bring you glory as I follow each and every one of your holy precepts."

Matthew 3:11-12 MSG, "I am baptizing you here in the river, turning your old life in for a kingdom life. The real action comes next: the main character Jesus in this drama-compared to him, I am a mere stagehand-will ignite the kingdom within you, a fire within you, changing you from the inside out. He is going to clean house make you a clean sweep of your lives. He will place everything true in its proper place before God, everything false he will put with the trash to be burned."

Foreword

In the time we live, believers are constantly engaged in spiritual warfare. This book exposes the enemy and helps us stay on guard against the tactics and the forces that the enemy uses against us. Spiritual warfare never ceases in the believer's life, and "The Unseen War: The Jezebel Afflicted Soul" helps us expose the enemy to stand against hell. Alena Moore takes us on a journey of her deliverance process and shares intimate moments of her healing process. God deposited revelation to her to equip the saints for various trials they would endure. Many believers are battling the orphan spirit and unforgiveness. This book will be a tool to help them obtain freedom through the Lord Jesus Christ.

Bishop Dr. Ron Webb

Table of Contents

Acknowledgements

I would like to acknowledge and thank the following people:

My husband Kevin: my best friend, the love of my life. Thank you for choosing me to share your life with, out of everyone else out there. You have always been one of my biggest supporters and encouragers to follow my heart after God. You have believed in me without measure and I am forever grateful for that. Our love and devotion for each other has always been our saving grace in difficult times. Thank you for being strong when I am weak and never giving up when we could have thrown in the towel. I believe the best is yet to come.

My children, daughters-in-law and grandchildren: you are the jewels in my crown, and my greatest accomplishments in this life besides this book. Thank you for reminding me of everything I taught you about God during one of the hardest times of my life. It was a beautiful thing! A kiss from heaven. You will forever be an example of the legacy I leave behind and my heart couldn't be any happier that God gave each one of you to me.

Bishop Ron Webb: Spiritual father, mentor and friend! Thank you from the bottom of my heart for recognizing the call of God on my life and obeying God to help me find my way. Thank you for encouraging and pushing me continually to stay engaged and finish the book when I wanted to give up. Thank you for helping me to complete this assignment and mandate on my life. I'm blessed to call you friend.

Pastor Shirley Winford: Our leader of Cleansing Streams, spiritual mentor and friend. Thank you for being deeply rooted in the word of God and being an example of Jesus on the earth. You have always shown me the love of God and I am forever grateful for that. You believed in me and stood up for me when so many others turned their backs on me and I love you for that.

Cleansing Streams: Founded by Paul and Rebecca Berndt, I would not have the freedom I have today without this ministry. It's a healing and deliverance ministry that teaches you the principles and the concepts to live by in the Word of God. I have been able to help teach and share so much of the knowledge I've gained from the content of this ministry. I have learned to put into practice so many life-changing concepts that have been essential to the freedom of many.

Pam Shell: my spiritual mom, "Not on my watch." Thank you, Pam, for always telling me the "truth" and not just what I wanted to hear. You have always held me accountable to walk in the Spirit and not the flesh. I wouldn't have the spiritual growth I do if it weren't for you kicking me in the tail when I needed it! Everyone needs a true friend like you. Forever blessed to be your friend.

My friends, family, and those strangers whom God has had interceding and praying for me while I was under some of the most ferocious attacks of my life while writing this book. A special thank you to Nicole, who spent countless hours helping me, including everyone else who helped me work on the content of this book. It has been a huge undertaking for my first book and I am blessed to have your support and help. It's taken an army! Thank you Carlen and Micheal for allowing me to share your testimonies for the advancing of the kingdom.

Hannah Moore for working with me on designing the perfect cover for this book. You did a beautiful job. Thank you for all of your help along the way! I couldn't have done it without your help and skills.

A big huge shout out to all the haters and betrayers; I would not have gained the knowledge and wisdom I needed to write this book without you. There will always be people in life who treat you wrong. When people treat you poorly, don't allow their bitterness to change who you are. Just keep being you! Some people cannot handle the level of anointing you have in Christ, but that's okay because some people will get you and they will understand. Sincerely, I thank each one of you for pushing me to destiny. I pray God's blessings on you!

Introduction

ILLEGITIMATE CURSE

The war over my life began upon conception. I was born out of wedlock and branded by demonic forces with an illegitimate curse and an orphan spirit from birth. I was unaware of the enemy's assignment against my life until a few years ago. The enemy plotted my destruction my entire life, but God had a plan to reverse the curse! When you are born out of wedlock, it does not make you less valuable to God, and His love for you is unchanging. However, for the curse to be broken, we must repent of the sin in our bloodline. The cross of Jesus Christ cuts off all curses flowing downstream, so we can break and reverse the curse to turn our bloodline back to God. Will you be a history maker for your bloodline?

The scripture below recounts God's unfailing love for us. We must learn to pass from curses to blessings. (Derek Prince) Unbeknownst to me, I had praying grandparents. My great-grandfather was a preacher, and because of his DNA in my bloodline, the power of the Holy Spirit drew me to receive a spiritual inheritance from God. That is where the battle began.

We have free will, but we must choose God's plan for our life. The enemy has legal ground to set you up because of the sin in your bloodline. He plans to keep you from your inheritance and from fulfilling your destiny. We are created by God and drawn by His Spirit to receive eternal life. Upon receiving Jesus Christ, the battle intensifies, and we step onto the frontlines of the battlefield. The devil throws everything at you he can to discourage you, fill you with despair, and steal your hope, so you will give up and throw in the towel. We are to be God's voice, making the invisible realm visible. God has given us power from Heaven to overcome the enemy.

The enemy is subservient to Yahweh. An unclean spirit, a fallen angel who rebelled against God. Satan, also known as the devil, or sometimes Lucifer in Christianity, is an entity in the Abrahamic religions that seduces humanity into falsehoods. He has temporary power in the earth, with a host of demons in a fallen world.[1]

Revelation 12:12-19, "and the great dragon was thrown down, that ancient serpent, who is called the devil and Satan the deceiver

1. "Satan." Wikipedia. Wikimedia Foundation, May 3, 2022. https://en.wikipedia.org/wiki/Satan.

of the whole world. He was thrown down to earth and the angels who followed him were thrown down with him."

So many people live defeated lives without power from the Holy Spirit. So, I hope to bring awareness to the unseen war and restore hope in the one true and living God. To reveal that no matter what you go through, God loves you and wants the absolute best for your life. Your relationship with God will determine your outlook on life. It will determine how you view and receive the Word of God, His faithfulness, goodness, and love. *To know love is to know God because He is love. (1 John 4:8)*

I have spoken with many people who cannot feel or see God's love in their circumstances. At the beginning of my journey, I didn't have a great perception of the Lord. It was difficult to feel His love because I couldn't see what He was doing in me and through me. It took some time and a lot of healing to realize that I was on the road to glory, and my Heavenly Father wanted me healed from the wounds of past generations and brokenness.

Psalm 121:1-8 TPT, "I look up to the mountains and hills, longing for God's help. But then I realized that our true help and protection is only from the Lord, our creator, who made the heavens and the earth. He will guard and guide me, never letting me stumble or fall. God is my keeper; He will never forget nor ignore me. He will never slumber nor sleep; He is the guardian-God for His people, Israel. Yahweh Himself will watch over you; He's always at your side to shelter you safely in His presence. He's protecting you from all danger both day and night. He will keep you from every form of evil or calamity as he continuously watches over you. You will be guarded by God himself.

You will be safe when you leave your home, and safely you will return. He will protect you now, and He'll protect you forevermore!"

The Holy Spirit is your lifeline to the Father. First, I had to learn who the Father was, along with Jesus Christ and the Holy Spirit. Then, I had to learn the voice of God, learn to hear Him, and obey His promptings and His Word. On this highway to holiness, we are to learn to walk in the Spirit of the Lord and not our fleshly desires. To do so, you must give up your fleshly desires, all the old ways of the world.

My flesh had to die to self and all the sin I had been living in. I couldn't keep doing whatever I wanted. I wanted to seek the truth and obey God. True obedience unto the Lord must become your lifestyle! A heart truly surrendered to the Lord will always seek the truth. On this journey, follow the Holy Spirit, who will lead you and guide you in all truth. Your obedience will move the heart of God! The Lord has made my life a living testimony of this war and taught me how to overcome as I partnered with the Holy Spirit.

God will use everything in your life, no matter what you have done, or how painful it is. He will show you how to count it all joy. So many of us have gone through difficulties in this life. That experience qualifies us to help others along their journey. I can't explain in words how many people I have helped because of what I have learned. Broken vessels yielded to God become healed vessels He can use. So let us surrender old mindsets, old ways, and patterns. *Greater is He that is in you than He that is in the world. (1 John 4:4)*

The only way we can fail is for us to give up and forfeit the call of God for our lives. The enemy cannot stop your purpose in the kingdom of God. You will have victory God's way! Please understand that the Lord is battling for you, cutting the cords that entangle. Often, we blame God for the mishaps and misfortunes in our lives, but have you considered everything He has already protected you from?

There is no greater rescuing power than the One who came for you and me. Together we will overcome as we partner with all of Heaven to confront the forces of evil that bombard us upon receiving Jesus Christ as our Lord and Savior. As we begin this journey to freedom, let us make a difference in this generation and those to come. We must rise as ambassadors of Christ.

We are to help encourage others not to give up along the way. Our responsibility is to teach the younger generations who God is and how to have a loving relationship with Him. He is faithful; we can have the abundant life He promised as our inheritance. So keep an open mind and ask your Heavenly Father to reveal all that you can't see in your life.

"We must not allow the next generation to walk into the abyss not knowing who Jesus Christ is or how to have a relationship with a Holy God. So many Christians are experiencing a lack of value, a loss of their purpose, loss of God's power, and lack of God's protection in their lives. If we sleep and do nothing, we are failing the future generations from a genuine encounter with God. We must protect the presence of the Lord and teach others how to experience and encounter him." (Pat Schatzline Rebuilding the Altar)[2]

We are called to become God's voice in the unseen realm. We are called to be a voice, to make the unseen seen. You only struggle with what you do not see. The god of this age, Satan, blinds people's minds resulting in them not being able to see the glory of Christ. The Lord is tearing down the barriers to the unseen realm and making them seen.

In the pages that lie ahead, I am transparent in expressing everything that I have been through in my life because I had to walk alone for so long on the road to glory. My heart desires to expose the enemy of your soul. There were many times when I felt abandoned and all alone, with no hope in sight. I would see other people seemed to find the happiness I lacked in my life but desperately desired. I knew there had to be more to this life we are living, and I set out to figure it out.

God drew me and set me on the path to destiny, but it wasn't until I surrendered that I saw the unseen war I had been fighting. I had to trust the Holy Spirit to gain insight into the demonic forces waging war against humanity. I believe every person comes to this place in their journey where they must come to the end of themselves and allow the process to fulfill the promises of God.

---

2. Schatzline, Pat, and Karen Schatzline. Rebuilding the Altar: A Bold Call for a Fresh Encounter with God. Lake Mary, FL: Charisma House, 2017, p. 119, paragraph 1.

I'm not looking for pity from pouring out my heart and soul in this book. The power of God in the life of an afflicted soul is something I want people to understand. A heart that is completely sold out and submitted to the Lord. You are fighting for your future generations. Becoming stuck and hitting the same wall for years is because of a lack of surrender. The scriptures below gives an account that God knows all about us, and He is always there! He never leaves.

Scriptures to consider: *Psalms 139:1-5 KJV*

1 "O lord, thou hast searched me, and known me."

2 "Thou knowest my downsitting and mine uprising, thou understandest my thought afar off."

3 "Thou compassest my path and my lying down, and art acquainted with all my ways."

4 "For there is not a word in my tongue, but, lo, O Lord, thou knowest it altogether."

5 "Thou hast beset me behind and before, and laid thine hand upon me."

CHAPTER 1

The Unseen War Between Two Kingdoms

The unseen realm is where the battle rages between two kingdoms: The Kingdom of Heaven and hell. The Bible tells us in *Genesis 1:1 KJV, "In the beginning God created the heaven and the earth."* And *2 Peter 2:4, "For if God spared not the angels that sinned, but cast them down to hell, and delivered them into chains of darkness, to be reserved unto judgment...."* We have the freedom to choose between these two kingdoms, but we must make a choice.

What will you choose, life or death, blessings or curses? There is no gray area. We cannot sit on the fence between the two. The time is upon us; we can no longer waver between two kingdoms. We are a chosen generation for such a time as this *(1 Peter 2:9)*. The end-time battle is upon us. Do you feel the pressures of the war between good and evil on the earth? We must take our heavenly place *(Colossians 2:12, Ephesians 2:6)*.

As a child of God you are the lineage of Christ, the lion of the tribe of Judah fully equipped, ready for battle, and not backing down. There are warriors on the horizon arising in the army of the Lord. A clarion call to battle has sounded. The Spirit of the living God has summoned a chosen generation! Will you awaken and arise to answer the call? Will you challenge the enemy? Will you stand in faith and take your rightful place in the kingdom of God to rule and reign?

I have the greatest news. Jesus has already won *(Revelation 1:18)*! We are fighting a war that was already won on the cross. Some people look at the cross in defeat, but God meant the cross for a much greater eternal purpose. Do you know who Jesus is? The Bible teaches us in *Exodus 15:3,6, KJV, "The Lord is a man of war: The Lord is His name.... Thy right hand, O Lord is become glorious in power: thy right hand, O Lord, hath dashed in pieces the enemy."*

When you accept Jesus as your Lord and savior, two things happen. First, you will have your own cross to bear. Jesus tells us in *Luke 9:23, NKJV, "If anyone desires to come after me, let him deny himself, and take up his cross daily, and follow me."* Second, you will have everything you need to fight this spiritual battle that rages in the heavens and on earth. Remember, you do not struggle for your soul only, but for others as well. The struggle between heaven and hell is for nothing less than the souls of humanity.

The enemy is like a roaring lion seeking to see whom he can devour. *(1 Peter 5:8)* The devil was attacking me before my salvation, but his attacks increased when I gave my life to the Lord. I had a false perception that everything should get easier. There is always a fight that God allows in order for us to grow our faith and trust Him. The Lord was with me in every battle, working out every detail. He protected me so much more than I knew or deserved. He was working out something far greater than I could see or imagine. I want to teach you how to fight these spiritual battles. The Bible tells us, in *1 Timothy 6:12 KJV, "Fight the good fight of faith, lay hold on eternal life, whereunto thou art also called, and hast professed a good profession before many witnesses."*

We must learn to fight from a place of victory and eternal life. Remember, we are fighting from our heavenly kingdom, which cannot be stopped! We cannot lose! I soon learned I was in bondage to the lies of the enemy. The weight of the war was so overwhelming heavy that victory seemed unattainable. I had developed a victim mindset that kept me defeated because of a lifetime of spiritual warfare. However, as God's children, the blood of the Lamb redeems us.

We are more than conquerors in Christ Jesus (*Romans 8:1*). It is necessary to learn who we are in Christ. When we become a son or daughter in God's army, He calls us to a life of a well-equipped, well-trained warrior. However, our training, guided by the Holy Spirit, is of the spirit and not of the flesh. We must learn to surrender and fully submit to the Holy Spirit. As a new follower of Christ, it seemed like surrendering was so easy, yet I would make it so difficult and frustrating. I had not yet learned that my flesh had to die daily to surrender fully. Life had already beaten me up. I didn't trust anyone. It was hard for me. The Lord will fight for us when we are obedient and fully surrender to Him.

Being prideful, fighting in your own strength, and doing everything in fleshly ways will only bring delays, weariness, and a burden too heavy to carry. I know many in the body of Christ are worn out from the battle not only within themselves, but also with the devil.

The Father showed me that the hearts of many Christians have grown cold. They give up because of the suffocating oppression, depression, and frustration. It frustrates them because their circumstances are not changing. They are looking for relief and breakthrough, but they are ignorant of the war they are in, which most cannot understand or refuse to discern. A lack of discernment is keeping the church in the dark. Many Christians think God is against them because of their sin, shortcomings, or failures.

When looking at the world, people take information from everywhere, process it, and then choose what to do with it. Some people seem to do nothing with what they see and learn. Others seem to take in their surroundings and are one step ahead of them. They make smart decisions. They have an almost supernatural ability to determine who is trustworthy or seem to always have the perfect advice for a situation.

They seem to have unique wisdom. This gift is called discernment, and it is a kind of wisdom that comes from insight as much as from learned experience and knowledge. In the Christian faith, it comes from the Holy Spirit and is a way of determining the true nature of a person, thing, or place. People with a spiritual gift of discernment have it, though wisdom and discernment can be bestowed to those who ask for it as well.

Discernment is a tool God gives believers as they walk through life, though it must be understood and the believer must follow the Lord's leading to be useful. In the simplest terms, discernment is wisdom. The dictionary just defines discernment as "the quality of being able to grasp and comprehend what is obscure; skill and discerning; an act of perceiving or just starting something." In the Christian faith, it is a similar concept, but it is bestowed by the Holy Spirit. Many denominations believe it can allow someone to know whether a demonic or heavenly influence is over a person, place, or event. It is also a gift that can be requested, used, or ignored.[3]

The enemy conducts a relentless assault on our mind, character, and identity in Christ.

---

3. Verrett, Bethany. "Understanding the Spiritual Gift of Discernment." biblestudytools. com. Salem Web Network, November 15, 2020. https://www.biblestudytools.com/ bible-study/topical-studies/understanding-the-spiritual-gift-of-discernment.html.

We lose faith when we do not understand who we are as God's children. We believe the lies and accusations against our minds. Some can discern the war in their spirit. They feel the opposition holding them back and pressing them down. However, they do not know the generational curses in their bloodline or evil spirits attacking them.

The biggest problem I was facing was that I did not understand what or who was opposing me. It was so confusing. I did not understand the authority of these invisible forces. I was unaware of my authority and did not know what that meant. I didn't know I had spiritual weapons or how to use them against the enemy. Sin had me at a disadvantage and my choices kept me in the dark. Because I was in the dark, I could not see the satanic structure I was up against, how it applied to my life in the natural, or how the enemy continually used people against me.

Early in my life, I learned to fight physically and verbally; it was all I had known. It was the only way I knew to survive. The enemy works continually to set us up because he works on our demise from an incredibly young age. I always felt this weight holding me back. I tried so hard to find the right strategy to get free, but I would just get frustrated and weary from battling in the natural realm instead of the spiritual realm.

When the battle is raging around you fiercely in the natural realm, it is extremely hard to comprehend what is going on in the spiritual realm.

There was a time when I had never heard of the spiritual realm. I had so much to learn. One tactic the enemy uses to distract us is to keep our focus on ourselves and off God. Jesus should always be our focus.

The Bible teaches us in *Ephesians 6:12-13, NKJV, (New Spirit-Filled Bible) says, "We wrestle not with flesh and blood; but with the principalities, against powers, against the rulers of darkness of this age, against spiritual hosts of wickedness in the heavenly places. Therefore, take up the whole armor of God that you may be able to withstand."*

To withstand means to "vigorously oppose, bravely resist, standing face to face against an adversary."[4] The authority and weapons necessary to "withstand" evil forces in spiritual warfare are available to us. Even with that knowledge, I did not understand the war I was in or the battle I was fighting. I cowered beneath the influence of the enemy and isolated myself, trying to avoid the battle. Like it or not, there is a war raging between the angelic and the demonic forces over the human soul.

There is a war going on between our flesh and our spirit. This battle rages within us as our two natures conflict with each other. Our relationships, minds, health, and bodies are under attack. There is a war on our faith, joy, and peace. There is a war on your finances, destiny, and spiritual inheritance. The war the enemy wages is the systematic destruction of all humankind.

---

4. www.dictionary.com. 2022. Definition of withstand | Dictionary.com. [online] Available at: <https://www.dictionary.com/browse/withstand> [Accessed 20 March 2022].

When we refuse to engage in the war, it is not pleasing to the Lord and opens a door for the enemy to bring more destruction upon us. We have no choice but to fight; there is too much complacency in the church. When we operate in the flesh, we cater to the forces of evil, which are trying to bring us down. Do not lose heart in the battle; there is greatness waiting for each one of us! Every single person can stand against the enemy and make a difference.

Keep eternity in your heart. Your life will become your message. When the enemy overplays his hand against your life, it is because he knows the greater glory that is coming to you. Satan and God are in a battle for the hearts of man; which kingdom will prevail? Let us partner with the Kingdom of God in our lives.

In the following scripture, I am giving biblical revelation to help bring light to the war I am referencing.

Consider 2 Corinthians 4:1-18 (NIV New Spirit-Filled Life Bible).
The light of the gospel

[1] Therefore, since through God's mercy we have this ministry, we do not lose heart. [2] Rather, we have renounced secret and shameful ways; we do not use deception, nor do we distort the word of God. On the contrary, by setting forth the truth plainly we commend ourselves to everyone's conscience in the sight of God. [3] And even if our gospel is veiled, it is veiled to those who are perishing. [4] The god of this age has blinded the minds of unbelievers, so that they cannot see the light of the gospel that displays the glory of Christ, who is the image of God. [5] For what we preach is not ourselves, but Jesus Christ as Lord,

and ourselves as your servants for Jesus' sake. ⁶ For God, who said, "Let light shine out of darkness," made his light shine in our hearts to give us the light of the knowledge of God's glory displayed in the face of Christ.

Cast down but not conquered

⁷ But we have this treasure in jars of clay to show that this all-surpassing power is from God and not from us. ⁸ We are hard pressed on every side, but not crushed; perplexed, but not in despair; ⁹ persecuted, but not abandoned; struck down, but not destroyed. ¹⁰ We always carry around in our body the death of Jesus, so that the life of Jesus may also be revealed in our body. ¹¹ For we who are alive are always being given over to death for Jesus' sake, so that his life may also be revealed in our mortal body. ¹² So then, death is at work in us, but life is at work in you.¹³ It is written: "I believed; therefore I have spoken." Since we have that same spirit of faith, we also believe and therefore speak, ¹⁴ because we know that the one who raised the Lord Jesus from the dead will also raise us with Jesus and present us with you to himself. ¹⁵ All this is for your benefit, so that the grace that is reaching more and more people may cause thanksgiving to overflow to the glory of God.

Seeing the invisible

¹⁶Therefore we do not lose heart. Though outwardly we are wasting away, yet inwardly we are being renewed day by day. ¹⁷ For our light and momentary troubles are achieving for us an eternal glory that far outweighs them all. ¹⁸ So we fix our eyes not on what is seen, but on what is unseen, since what is seen is temporary, but what is unseen is eternal.

The providential hand of God was controlling Paul's persecutions, keeping them within manageable proportions. Paul enlarges the theme of power through weakness to include life through the death of the fleshly soulish realm. Paul's mission was dangerous. He endured and suffered many hardships and surrendered himself to his probable death. However, during perils, he could experience the life of Jesus, strengthening and sustaining him in his present weakness and assuring him of the future resurrection. Paul suffered hardship so that we could know the power of God. Earthen vessels are fragile. This verse is vertically thematic for the entire letter, expressing the paradox of how weak human beings can be the instruments of the power of God.

Compared to the eternal weight of glory, Paul's hardships are only light afflictions *(Romans 8:18)*. The transcendent glory of the ministry of the New Covenant provides the basis for courage, therefore, take courage my friends and do not lose heart because of faith in the future resurrection. Also, because of the present experience of God's renewing power, Paul continues to preach with courage and determination.

There is tremendous treasures in the face of Jesus. Do not keep focusing on the temporal things, but the eternal. Take a glimpse into the hoped for, yet unseen. Look directly into the eyes of faith, where so many cannot see!

CHAPTER 2

A Look Inside From One Who Sees

I would like to share a deliverance experience that illustrates the warfare I am describing. A young man named Michael, whom I met at church, was struggling with demonic oppression. The church put together a team to help free him from this demonic abuse. Some of the church leaders asked me to be a part of this team. So, with his permission, I share a part of his story.

As a child and young teenager, Michael learned about church and God from his family. He said what he was missing was a relationship with Jesus; he did not know Him as Lord until later in life. He attended a youth group and gave his life to the Lord at 13, although he did not realize what he was doing.

Michael said he always remembered being pulled to the supernatural. He always felt a drawing to explore the unseen and unknown. A sense of curiosity kept him searching for the paranormal. The ghost stories were very intriguing. There were television shows that highlighted this paranormal activity that kept him infatuated. The enemy seduced him with a familiar spirit. The enemy learns about your life through familiar spirits, generational curses, and the things that you speak out of your mouth. The devil sets up a false identity to keep you from fulfilling your eternity in Christ. If you do not know the truth about God and His ways, it is difficult to understand the importance of these spiritual gifts.

Someone often leads people astray because of a poor foundation on God's Word. The enemy twists your purpose and spiritual gifts to get you so far off track, hoping that you cannot return or recover. Michael has a powerful gift of discerning of spirits, along with the seer and prophetic gifts, allowing him to see into the unseen spiritual realm.

The enemy knew when he was young and unaware exactly how to lead him astray. Many parents today are unaware that witchcraft is luring their children in little by little with kid shows that are introducing witchcraft, spells, and magic wands, etc. It takes someone strong to stand up and be an advocate for God and speak the truth to them in love. Too many refuse to see the truth and take a stand. Kids are being lured in by the seeds of witchcraft unbeknownst to them or their parents.

Kids with the gift of discernment and prophecy are extremely sensitive to the spiritual realms. They can sense what is going on in the natural and spiritual realm. They can hear from God easily, but are not aware unless they have a strong spiritual mentor and guidance. Children are often under spiritual attack from the enemy at a young age. He tries to confuse them and trick them into darkness. That is exactly what happened to Michael and countless others. The enemy created a false image of something harmful making it appear to be good in order to entice and lure many astray. A plumbline is a standard used to measure the difference between good and evil. God's plumbline is a standard of holiness, righteousness, and justice. God created a measure of righteous for us to live by. It's a reference line to measure our lives by so we are not led astray. A false plumbline is the opposite of all that is good. It's the opposite of God's standards and justice.[5]

Marketed and sold as a kid's game, the Ouija board is a perfect example. This game is extremely bad and it can open a door to negative spiritual activity. A child doesn't know that this "toy" can actually lead to releasing demonic forces. Once Michael played the Ouija board with some friends, it opened a demonic portal that released paranormal activity with demonic spirits. In the beginning, this excited Michael because of the power he could sense and feel. That is how the enemy starts out, getting you involved and then turning on you.

5. "Plumb-Line- Are You All Measured up for God? – Amos 7." Biblical Thoughts, April 19, 2015. https://talkativeangel.wordpress.com/2014/07/08/plumb-line-are-you-all-measured-up-for-god-amos-7/.

Michael said he became very rebellious toward his family and would not listen to them when they tried to help him. When Michael was in his early twenties, he was told by his parents that he was sexually abused by a babysitter's son. He felt like this was a great betrayal because they kept the truth from him for so long. He thought they should have told him sooner because of the struggles he endured and this opened the door for a deeper rebellion in him. His defiance led to his not caring what anyone thought or said. Rebellion led him away from God and his Christian upbringing. The more he experienced the demonic realm, the more he heard the conversations of the demon spirits. The more it happened, the more he could not control it. Ultimately, he became trapped in alcohol abuse and mind-altering drugs.

If the enemy can get you into an altered state of mind, he can use you more in witchcraft without your awareness. These things set Michael on a road to destruction, and his life spiraled out of control. He would do things he really did not want to do because he knew it hurt his family, but he would do it anyway.

He later learned that he was living with a generational curse of sorcery passed down in his bloodline on his father's side. His great-great grandmother and great-grandmother were involved in witchcraft. That is how curses can affect future generations to the 4th and 5th generations. That curse was pulling and drawing him to the dark side. Michael inherited a false kundalini spirit, which is a false Holy spirit, through generational sorcery.

The kundalini spirit is derived from the Hindu religion. This religion promotes an awakening of inner energy and self-glorification. Through Yoga, mind meditations and certain poses and movements are dedicated to other gods. This is designed to awaken a coiled snake in the base of the spine. The spiritual awakening is geared toward an individual's promotion of self-energy and identity. Satan uses one's mind to appeal to the desires of one's flesh. He feeds the mind to receive lies and believe they are true. In this deception, he can get them to act upon their own feelings, desires, and excitement. This leads us to error and into false doctrine. Self-centered desires are without God-centered activities. Our function is to obey and fulfill the Word of God and wholly depend upon the influence of the Holy Spirit to transform our lives into the image of Christ. According to the Word of God, the Holy Spirit speaks to our spirit and not our flesh or the promotions of our own will and fleshly desires. The Holy Spirit doesn't glorify himself and acts only to glorify the person of Jesus Christ. The true anointing of the Holy Spirit is sovereign. The Holy Spirit can only honor His own truth. The real cause of the loss of the extraordinary gifts of the Holy Spirit is because the hearts of many has waxed cold. The hearts of many are searching and searching. They are finding themselves in spiritism and witchcraft, therefore, being led astray in their belief of self desire and self glorification.[6] False evidence appearing real. The kundalini spirit comes from the ancient practice of yoga. Most Christians do not want to believe this, but it is a fact. If you do your research, you can find the truth easily.

---

6. "Downloads – Kanaan Ministries." Accessed May 11, 2022. https://www.kanaanministries.org/downloads/.

Eventually, the drugs landed Michael in jail. In jail, he found Jesus Christ, while reflecting on his younger years and remembering going to church. That, my friends, is the true Holy Spirit leading him back to God.

The Lord never forgot about Michael making a commitment that day long ago. He never left him and was there the entire time with His love and mercy, saving him from more than he will ever know on this side of Heaven. We all have free will to choose the path we take, but eventually God brings us back to Himself to fulfill the call of destiny He has for us. Receiving Jesus does not mean you will not have consequences for your sin. You will still reap the consequences. After recommitting his life to Jesus, and really meaning it with all his heart, his spiritual gift of seeing in the Spirit fully opened.

That is when the battle between Heaven and hell ramped up in his life. The curse is still in effect until broken. Have no fear, the Holy Spirit will lead you to break all curses. My goal is to bring to light the deception that religious people believe, which is when you are a Christian, you instantly should be perfect.

There is a process on the highway towards holiness. Michael suffered many spiritual attacks against his life. There was a war raging in his body, mind, and soul. He had a lot of confusion and mental fog. He could not tell the difference between the real Holy Spirit and the false kundalini spirit.

He just wanted the torment to stop. When it didn't, he became suicidal. He was trying to fight his battle in the natural because he was unaware of another way to fight. It seemed nothing worked to his avail. Fear, stress, and anxiety took over his life. Once fear gets in, it has its own torment. The war against his life was very intense, and he was desperate for help. The only hope and godly help he knew at the time was the Lord's prayer. He would just repeat it over and over. He returned to church out of desperation for some relief.

Michael knew this situation was much bigger than he was, and God was his only help! He was ready to surrender it all to God... Finally! This brings us back to the deliverance session. There were four people in the room besides Michael. We prayed and asked questions to get some background to know what we were up against. Suddenly, Michael's spiritual eyes opened, and he told us he saw "little black dots and black shadows" everywhere. The shadows were blurry and shifting from place to place. He knew it was demonic activity. He could sense it in the atmosphere. All the darkness was taunting him and saying they would never leave.

As we prayed, he saw flashes of white and blue light all over the room. As we prayed and took authority over all darkness, warring angels appeared on the scene. He could see them blurring by quickly. I believe God allowed him to see the war going on in the atmosphere to bring him peace, to give us all courage, and to make us aware and to know Heaven was fighting for us all, no matter what it looked like in the natural. The light was consuming all the darkness in the room.

He'd seen a demonic spirit with the voice of a witch jump between him and me. It told him I did not have what it took to get rid of it. He repeated what it said out loud and I said that Jesus was the one that would get rid of it. I was just a willing vessel standing in faith. All a sudden, a bright light came down from the left and wiped out the darkness. Another flash of white light came in with a sword and literally sliced through the darkness and squashed it down. The light severed the dark shapes.

The light stopped the path of darkness in its tracks. The warring angels were fierce and mighty! Michael witnessed strikes of lightning during this battle. This should encourage you that His glorious light dispels all darkness! You have nothing to fear! The curse of witchcraft and sorcery was now broken. Michael and his future generations were now free. Michael's battle did not end that day. He is still learning as he walks with God. The Lord teaches you warfare and prayer as you grow and mature in Him! What a wonderful display of God's glory!

CHAPTER 3

The End Of Myself

I found myself on my knees at the altar, broken, and sobbing uncontrollably. The torment from the enemy, the weight of my sin and bad choices was more than I could bear. I was desperate for a God I barely knew. Unbeknownst to me, even as an incredibly young girl, I was being drawn and led by the power of the Holy Spirit. *Jeremiah 31:3, "I have loved you with an everlasting love; therefore, with loving kindness I have drawn you."* I was at the end of myself.

That morning, I visited a Spirit-filled, nondenominational church. I was being pushed and prodded by the Holy Spirit, people, and my circumstances. Some by my design, some by the hand of the Lord. The power of the Holy Spirit touched me. I felt His presence so strongly I cried out, "God help me, I feel so alone. I am so alone." Through my tears of pain, I heard Him say... "You are not alone, for I am always with you." This was something I had previously heard at church but had not felt or experienced in a long time.

In the following chapters, the orphan spirit will be explained in greater detail. Abandonment and rejection had infiltrated my heart through that orphan spirit, leaving me feeling isolated from everyone. I have since learned that isolation is a ploy of the enemy to overwhelm you, get you to doubt the goodness of God and the truth of His love for those in His Word. This is the true essence of God's identity. I struggled with the isolation on and off for many years because I allowed the enemy to push me around, not realizing I was in a war I knew nothing about. The war on my mind was relentless day and night. I could barely think straight. In my late teenage years, I fell away from church and God. I could always feel Him there with me, trying to keep me on the right path.

I learned about religion, but nothing about a relationship with Jesus. A relationship is truly what is in the heart of the Father. That is why He sent Jesus to redeem us back to Him. I continued to hold on to this scripture throughout my life when-ever I would go through bouts of loneliness. *Isaiah 41:10 KJV, "Fear thou not; for I am with thee; be not dismayed; for I am thy God: I will strengthen thee; yea, I will help thee; yea I will uphold thee with the right hand of righteousness."*

I would remind the enemy that I was not alone because the Lord was with me. This is part of the mind battle; the enemy lies to you, and you must counter with the truth, which is the word of God. God is always with us through the Holy Spirit, who dwells on the inside of us. Unfortunately, it took my brokenness to bring me back to the Lord, the altar, and a place of covenant.

God knew my scars would have a story to tell.

Your scars will have a story to tell. There are people only you can reach. He is counting on you to do your part. He is raising the broken-hearted back to life, lifting them up out of the ashes to the "Great Awakening" of the sons and daughters.

We must be willing vessels on the journey (process) leading us along the highway to holiness, which leads to Jesus. Holiness leads us to the glory! I know your past is broken but you can move on now. Choose to let it go, and allow the healing process to begin. See yourself as Christ sees you.

SALVATION

At church that morning, I experienced my first encounter with Jesus Christ. It was my first awareness of the Savior. But who was this Savior? What exactly did salvation mean? To be honest, I could feel rebellion in my flesh revolting against Jesus, not wanting to accept Him, and I did not know why. This is when I realized the war between my spirit and my flesh. My flesh was bitter and full of anguish, not wanting to submit, only to rebel and resist Jesus. I loved God, but I did not know Jesus or the Holy Spirit. At church, my spirit leaped, as it was being refreshed, renewed, and brought to life. It was the first time I felt at home. I had experienced God a long time ago as a young child (age 4-5). I remember going to Vacation Bible School and feeling this awesome feeling of God's presence. We were singing songs about the Lord, not realizing He was the Savior of our souls, the Savior of the world. We sang, "Jesus Loves Me" and "Kumbaya my Lord." Kumbaya means "Come by here." The song says: "Kumbaya, Kumbaya my Lord. Oh Lord Kumbaya, someone's crying Lord, Kumbaya my Lord."

Little did I know those lyrics would stay with me throughout my life. Little did I know, as I would sing, I was asking the Lord to come by here, come by me. I never forgot that night at Vacation Bible School and feeling God's touch that day. As a 4th-5th grader, I went to church often alone. The rest of my family went very little, if at all. The Holy Spirit continued to draw me to the church. I helped in the nursery and candle lighting until I was in high school.

Salvation prayer: "I come to you with a humble heart, in the name of Jesus. I realized that I have been living life for myself, a life of sin, which is serving the devil, and not you. I have been living a life that is not pleasing to you, Lord. I have been living ungodly. I repent and turn away from those things now. I want to desire the life you desire for me, and stop serving myself and the devil. I can't do this on my own, Jesus. I ask you into my heart now and I declare you are my Lord and Savior. You now may rule in my life. Change me, Lord, cleanse me and heal me your way.

I declare Jesus is now my Lord and the Son of God. Thank you, Jesus, for rescuing my soul and changing my life. Amen."

BETRAYALS

I had a very dysfunctional and unstable home life growing up. It was honestly one crushing betrayal after another. I grew up in an alcoholic home with a belligerent drunk. I found out around 12 years old during a physical fight between my parents that the man I thought was my dad was not my father. That was a very crushing blow for a young girl. That started me on a quest to find my biological father, which would span over most of my adult life. I was then told another man was my father, only to find out he was not my dad either. I discovered this through taking an Ancestry DNA test.

There was so much rebellion, control, manipulation, fear, stress, anxiety, strife, physical fighting, arguing, and mental anguish. When I was around 13 years old, a family member molested and harassed me. This same person harassed and pursued me until my second marriage. When I was in school, I desperately tried to talk to the counselor and those in authority, but no one took me seriously. I could not escape the fear and torment of it all. It was all so unbearable. As a result, my teenage years were filled with drinking alcohol to escape the pain.

I remember going to school drunk on more than one occasion. We would have parties and such. Thankfully, that never got too out of hand. I was looking for love in all the wrong places, which led to some sexual promiscuity. I did not know that I was acting out of those curses in my bloodline. I always had a void and emptiness I was trying to fill. Only God could fill the void and emptiness. The very people that were supposed to protect me accused me of so many unthinkable things. I was not an angel. I was rebellious and acted out, mostly trying to defend myself, crying out for someone to help me.

Church seemed to be a safe place. It was a place of peace I desperately needed. When you are growing up, you do not realize the magnitude of trauma faced in your life until you are in your 20, 30, or 40s. This is where the effects of your childhood are inescapable. I carried this over into my first marriage:

- anger
- rage
- violence
- hatred
- resentment
- unforgiveness
- loneliness
- revenge
- control
- rejection
- abandonment
- depression
- heaviness
- fear
- broken heartedness
- and a crushed spirit.

I was not a horrible person, although many looking at me may have thought that I was. My behavior reflected the trauma I experienced. I had to fight to survive and keep my head above water. Most people knew nothing about my issues. I was very misunderstood and that followed me throughout my life. I thought my first husband would rescue me from all the turmoil I was going through, but that was not the case. He just added to my destruction.

He promised me the world, only to break his promises and betray me which caused an even deeper brokenness in me. I had so much hope for the future, not realizing that it would lead to the darkest hours of my life. He ended up being a chronic cheater (a curse in his bloodline) which left me in utter despair. I was so discouraged and hopeless about life and the future. The first time I remember him cheating was when I was pregnant with my first son. A time that was supposed to be joyous was one of grief and sadness.

I had so many struggles during this time because of his cheating. It left me feeling so unworthy, unloved, abandoned, and rejected. It only reinforced every betrayal and lie the enemy used against me in childhood, and every insecurity I suffered from growing up resurfaced. It brought back all the fear, betrayal, rejection, and loneliness.

It seemed magnified at this point because I was being blamed for everything because of the anger and bitterness I had carried. At the end of our marriage, we had several separations and divorce filings. After 4 or 5 different girls, he left and moved in with one of them and they married. During those really dark and emotional times, I really did not know how I would make it. Some days it was difficult to get out of bed, but the love for my children and the provincial hand of God kept me going.

I was never suicidal, but still as lost as anyone could be. I was a stay-at-home mom that ended up with two jobs trying to make ends meet. This only added to my anger, hatred, revenge, and destruction. I did not even know what to do with all the bitterness I was feeling. I had so much anger; I was lashing out at anyone who got in my way. I really did not care anymore. I was numb and broken. I felt like I would never heal.

There is an unseen enemy working with force through the negative people in your life, working behind the scenes to bring you to utter destruction. He will use any willing vessel he can against you. I did not know this war was against me. I just could not understand it. I kept asking the Lord, "Why, why me?" What had I done so wrong? There was no rhyme or reason. It was during this time I fell into self-pity. I had learned a victim mentality.

The dark forces of the enemy were fighting against my prophetic gifting and call of destiny. They were trying to cause me to give up on life and to shut me down prophetically and emotionally. I have since learned that people cannot give you more than what they know or have. I had put my hope and trust in man instead of God. I honestly made my ex-husband an idol before God unknowingly. I was desperate for a better life. I had two small children (ages 3 and 1). I wanted a better life for them, better than what I had. I tried to hold on with all that I had, which left me exhausted.

A lack of knowledge of God's Word and His love does not keep you exempt from the war. I spent eight weeks in a stress center trying to cope with everything that had happened in my life. I know my parents gave all they had. Now, looking back, I can clearly see their brokenness and the addictions they were living with. They were trying to survive. I am thankful for everything that I learned because I can now share with others how to live and not just survive. I wish that I would have learned more before I passed some of the fear, stress, anxiety, strife, and arguing traits to my children.

Parents, every choice you make affects all your future generations.

I have been standing in the gap and partnering with the Holy Spirit to learn how to stop the Jezebel spirit. It only takes one generation to turn your bloodline away from God. You must engage in the battle God's way. There are generational curses in operation that most people are unaware of because it is not talked about much from the pulpit. They are real.

As I reflected on my life before that day in church, I often felt like I had no one to count on. I had people in my life, but I still had an emptiness in my heart. I surrendered and gave my life to the Lord Jesus. I gave Him all I had available that day. All the betrayal I experienced broke my heart. I was so numb that I could feel nothing. I could not feel God's love. I was incredibly sad, discouraged, hopeless, and full of pain.

God will shout at you through your pain. I had some deep-rooted wounds from my past and betrayals from the people whom I thought should love me and protect me the most. I did not know how to let go of them. I did not know how I would ever recover. I honestly did not even know I needed to recover and heal. This was affecting every area of my life. It was affecting every relationship. I was full of anger, rage, and bitterness. I was miserable and I wanted revenge for those who had hurt me.

Everyone around me, my husband, children, family, friends, and even what felt like God had hardened my heart. I was living and operating out of that woundedness. I kept everyone at arm's length! That isolation made me feel even more alone.

You cannot win your war from a place of isolation. Isolation is a tactic of the enemy to keep you separated from God, those who genuinely love you and those God has called to help you. We all need help on the journey because the battle is fierce.

I was living with an extremely poor image of myself. I felt unworthiness, rejection, abandonment, regret, and insecurity.

I did not know the meaning of a love that did not hurt.

The love of the Father was unknown to me. I did not trust anyone enough to let them in. I was just surviving. When I gave my life to the Lord, He began healing. The power of God can melt even the hardest and coldest of hearts. Little did I know, it would be a long journey. My life has been one of enduring and perseverance. Through repentance and forgiveness, I am now seeing more clearly.

I want to share my journey and God's process of bringing me from darkness into His marvelous light. My intention is to shed light on the relentless war of the Jezebel spirit against our souls, our identities, and our voices. The Jezebel Spirit is a principality/strongman that works and operates through unsuspecting individuals. Through my own experiences, I truly believe that most people have no idea what they are up against in dealing with this nasty, cunning, and pure evil spirit. Jezebel is not just one spirit. It is a compilation of the characteristics of many spirits. It is sly, sneaky, deceptive, controlling, and manipulative. It causes strife, destruction, and division in homes, families, churches, ministries, and businesses. This spirit operates through certain traits of individuals such as seduction, fear, evil foreboding, hatred, anger, and bitterness. It plays relentless mind games with you through these secondary spirits. As you fall prey and cooperate and participate with it by coming under it's demonic influence, it builds a demonic structure in your mind to control and manipulate every decision you make or don't make out of fear. It gains more leverage over your life through patterns and cycles of disobedience and rebellion to God. It will play the same mind games with you as long as they work. In order to overcome it, we must be humble, recognize the pride we are operating in, and repent. The war on our inheritance tries to keep us from fulfilling the prophetic call of destiny in our lives. On your journey, the Holy Spirit is leading you to destiny. One of the greatest wars we fight is between our spirit and our flesh. I want to expose how the spirit of Jezebel[7] runs rampant in a family until someone takes a stance to stop it.

You must be able to recognize it in order to stop it. I had absolutely no knowledge of Jezebel or the dark forces operating against me. Life seems to be harder for me than most people. I had become a battled weary soldier. I had found a love for God and wanted to give all my heart to Him at an incredibly young age and the enemy brought one assault after the other. Many do not see or understand the demonic forces and curses that are raging war against their body, soul, and spirit. Their mind, will, and emotions. I hope through sharing my painful journey and the wounds in my soul, that will help somebody get free. I hope to teach them to battle spiritually so they can learn who they are in Christ and become all that God has created them to be.

My prayer is for you to know the freedom that took years and years for me to find on the ancient path by following the Holy Spirit. Every Christian has their own war to fight. Like it or not, we are in a war. Every assault on your life pushes you and knocks you out of alignment with God and your destiny. Jesus has already won the victory, but we must wage war to set ourselves

7. Britannica, T. Editors of Encyclopaedia. "Jezebel." Encyclopedia Britannica, January 6, 2021. https://www.britannica.com/biography/Jezebel-queen-of-Israel.

and our generations free. As believers, God has equipped us with everything we need for the battle and victory. We will emerge from the ashes victorious if we allow God complete access by surrendering all we have.

I want to encourage you— the Lord hears your cry! Not every trial you face is from the enemy. God's hand is firmly upon you. He is searching for the depths of every heart that is shut up because it is leaving Him no access. In the battle you are facing, He is exposing the hidden areas of your heart that are keeping you from Him and all that He has for you. We must quit the prideful ways that are keeping us from a fulfilling relationship with Jesus. I was so full of pride; I was deceived because I thought I was protecting myself. It was a lie from the enemy that had a long history in my bloodline.

I did not know Jezebel was at work. Once I got saved, I thought, "Wow my life is about to get so much better."

Eternally, everything changed, but internally I had so much to learn and overcome.

I thought I would fight the enemy like I did everyone else in life. Warning... Big mistake! I experienced so much backlash because of my prideful attitude. Pride comes before the fall. I fell alright, right into the fiery furnace of the Lord. We must do away with the old man and come forth with the new.

It was very overwhelming and confusing to understand who the old man was and then try to figure out what the new man looked like. When you are in the fire, God is refining and purifying you from the past. This time is extremely uncomfortable and you are not sure about anything. You wrestle between the Holy Spirit and flesh. You are trying to take a stand against the past, but you do not realize what it is going to take to get to your destiny. So you quarrel with your Maker about what you want and how you think you should get there. A battle of wills begins. Your will and the will of the Father for your life.

When you are in the fire, it is exceedingly difficult to see the love of God. I could only see Him as a disciplinarian. In the Word, I would read about His love, but I could not feel it because the fire was intense. At the same time, I was trying to let go and hold on. I made it about works and performance because that was all I knew. I knew nothing about His grace. The old man and victim mentality were so deeply rooted in my identity. I was basing my entire identity on everything negative because that is exactly what the enemy wants you to believe, accusing you in your mind day and night. It is so vital that you stay engaged in the fire and let God work.

He must deliver you from the mess you have made. He must break down the false foundations erected by your former generations and continued by you so they do not affect any future generations. Even though God has forgiven us, our sin has consequences, and the effect of sin is still in your soul. Sin creates wounds in our souls. It can cause sickness in your body. Healing and deliverance are a process, which the enemy does not want to happen. So, he wars continually against your soul and the wounds there, trying to keep you in sin so he can destroy your life. One of my first life scriptures says:

"And we know that God causes all things to work together for good to those who love God, to those who are called according to His purpose." (Romans 8:28, NASB)

No matter how many bad choices you have made or sins you have committed on earth, we are all sinners on this side of Heaven. Sin will constantly be at war with your soul. God looks at all sin the same. Thankfully, He is a gracious, merciful, and a loving Father who works with us through our repentance. He is faithful and works all things together. That does not mean there are no consequences for your sin. Sin opens a door for the enemy to attack you. Therefore, it is so important to shut all doors of sin. The Holy Spirit is the fixer of the breach and the broken gates through our humility and surrender. The Father, through His mercy and grace, empowers us to overcome the enemy.

The war teaches you to stand firm under pressure because when you are under pressure, you discover the destiny that was placed on the inside of you. What is on the inside of you has already been determined to prevail. I tell you this, He who is in you is greater than any obstacle set before you. The Lord is teaching you to walk by the Holy Spirit and not your circumstances, not by what others say or by what the world says. The Lord orders the steps of the righteous.

When you stay humble before the Lord, He works a greater measure of faith through your circumstances. The Holy Spirit will hold firm to His plan, His timing, so His purposes will prevail. Before the beginning of time, God preordained your destiny. There is a book in Heaven that tells your story *(Psalm 139:13-16 NLT, Eph. 2:10, Is. 48:10).* You must partner with the Holy Spirit to complete the good work in you and fulfill the call of destiny. Ask Jesus to open your book. Every trial and experience you go through is preparing you for destiny, so do not doubt and forfeit your peace with worry, stress, and anxiety.

Trials and experiences create a greater compassion in you that will better equip you to minister to the hurting and lost people. Today, you must refuse to settle for less than what God has promised you. You cannot prevail in your own strength and might, but only by the Spirit of the living God.

Be confident in everything the Lord is working in your life during the process. Relinquish all control over to the Holy Spirit because the Lord is mighty, strong, and never changing. He will make all His grace abound toward you. Whatever He has started in you, He will finish. What He has prophesied over your life will manifest. Your perspective will change in your victories. The anointing and your authority will increase. Hope will arise as He sets forth His deliverance and sets you free from the strongholds and mindsets of the past.

Once the fog lifts, you will see more clearly.

CHAPTER 4

Christ, the Repairer

God hates evil. He hates sin. If He got rid of all evil in the world, He'd have to get rid of all of us. We all have evil and sin in our hearts. But God has a plan to get rid of all evil, one person at a time. He sent Jesus to the earth to fulfill that plan. Jesus paid the price of our sin, which is death, and died in our place, resulting in our redemption and restoration.

When we receive Jesus, God deposits the Holy Spirit in our hearts. The Holy Spirit cleanses our hearts from the inside out and gives us the power to resist evil. Although God is sovereign, He does not force His will upon us. He leaves our decisions up to us. He wants us to make the right decision, to use the authority He has given us to bring evil under control. He wants us to realize the devil's tactics, resist evil when we see it, separate ourselves from it, and make laws to control or eliminate it whenever it manifests itself.

Prayer is the primary means God gives us to combat and defeat away evil tactics of the enemy. God has set up certain laws on the Earth, and He will not violate them. For example, the laws of nature and the law of gravity are all laws that exist to keep order in the Earth. However, there are also laws of human nature, one of which is our free will. Even though God is all-powerful, He has given us control over what happens to us on the Earth. One of the most powerful means by which we control things on the Earth is through prayer. We pray and ask God to intervene. He acts in response to our asking. The prayers of those who believe and love Him are His primary tools for affecting our world. If we do not ask, there cannot be an answer. We allow evil to proliferate when we do not resist it or pray about it. We move out from under God's protective covering when we do not live His way and seek His protection.

Jesus said, "I will give you the keys of the kingdom of heaven; and whatever you bind on earth shall have been bound in heaven, and whatever you loose on earth shall have been loosed in heaven." *(Matthew 16:19, NASB95)* Binding and loosing have to do with forbidding and permitting. Through this kind of prayer, God has given us instructions for how to forbid evil from controlling our lives and permit God to be in charge. So why don't we pray this way?

One reason may be our unwillingness to acknowledge that evil exists or acknowledge our sin. Another might be that we are afraid of having Him interfere with our lives. Or maybe we do not believe that God cares about us or that prayer even works. However, when God is invited, He is always present. If we do not invite God into a situation or people's lives, He will not be there.

Indeed, God is everywhere, but He does not manifest His power when not consulted. When Jesus taught us how to pray, He gave us the Lord's prayer as a model. Our all-knowing God, who knows everything we need, tells us to ask for Our Daily Bread in that prayer. If He knows we need food, why does He still want us to ask for it? In that same prayer, our all-powerful God, who has the power to destroy evil in the blink of an eye, tells us to pray for deliverance from evil. Why does He do that? Because one of His principles is that we should ask, and He will answer.

God asked us to pray to Him for the things we need in our lives. He wants us to partner with Him to guide what happens on the Earth. If we need God to intervene in a situation and He is nowhere to be found, it is probably because no one asked Him to be there in power.

Whenever people want God to leave them alone, He will. If it seems like God is absent from a situation, it is our fault, not His. It is because we have not invited Him to be there in power. We must partner with God to bring His full power to bear in any situation, helping us overcome.[8]

We must be quick to repent from sin to be released from slavery to the evil one. Do it quickly and receive His new mercies

8. Omartian, S., 2002. The power of a praying nation. Eugene, Or.: Harvest House, p. 22, paragraph 2.

because you have become a new creature by accepting Him. Forgiveness is the key to unlocking the fear and pain of the past. Soon, you will understand all of your struggles. God doesn't just solve our earthly problems. He is concerned with the condition of our hearts. Where the Spirit of the Lord is, there is liberty!

CHAPTER 5

Repentance

The action of repentance is a sincere act of regret or re-morse.[9] You can only prosper from the discipline of reexamining your heart daily. We must take an inventory every day. Be willing to admit to anything that does not line up with the Word of God. We must submit to God and be truly sorry. It is not always easy to see our own heart condition or our own sin. It takes great courage and strength to confess the sin that has taken control of our lives.

When we diligently pursue the truth of the Word of God, it is a treasure. The Bible gives us this promise: repent now and God will forgive your sins. The refreshing newness of forgiveness can only come from the Lord *(Acts 3:19)*. If we do not repent, we can-not receive help and relief from the torment of sin.

9. www.dictionary.com. 2022. Definition of repentance | Dictionary.com. [online] Available at: <https://www.dictionary.com/browse/repentance> [Accessed 20 March 2022].

The Bible clearly tells us in *2 Peter 3: 9 NIV, "... the Lord is not slow in keeping his promise, as some understand slowness. Instead, he is patient with you, not wanting anyone to perish but everyone to come to repentance."* We must recognize, renounce, and repent. God loves when we recognize our sin, renounce partnering with sin, and repent. As Christians, confession must become an ongoing discipline. We change every day, little by little as we continue to recognize sin. We will grow spiritually as we submit to God. Allowing our fleshly desires to be crucified, we become more and more Christlike. Repentance is the best sign that we are growing deeply and rapidly in the character of Jesus.[10]

In owning and admitting the sin we have in our hearts, we are enabled to find freedom. To deny sin and resist truth is to remain stuck in the same destructive cycles and patterns. As we repent, the atonement of Jesus Christ becomes fully effective in our lives, and the Lord forgives our sins. We become free from the bondage of our sins, and we find peace and joy. When we submit to God by repenting, we proclaim we belong to God, and we can fight and resist the enemy and his evil influences. We choose to trust God, instead of who we are not. There is a difference between humility and pride. Pride will keep you from repenting. The opposite of pride is humility, meaning we agree with the truth. Perhaps that is why Paul says that repentance leads us to know the truth so that we can come to our senses. *(2 Timothy 2:25-26)*

---

10. Skones, S., Skones, S. and Skones, S., 2022. A Life of Repentance? — Living Word Fellowship. [online] Living Word Fellowship. Available at: <https://www.livingwf.org/news/2019/8/25/a-life-of-repentance> [Accessed 20 March 2022].

The Apostle John reminds us in *1 John 1:8-10 TPT, "If we boast that we have no sin, we are only fooling ourselves and are strangers to the truth. But if we freely admit our sins when light uncovers them, he will be faithful to forgive us every time. God is just to forgive us our sins because of Christ, and he will continue to cleanse us from all unrighteousness. If we claim we are not guilty of sin when God uncovers it with his light, we make him a liar and his word is not in us."* Salvation comes to every person who turns to God in genuine repentance and faith. There is a difference between repenting of a sin and pulling down the stronghold. The first involves faith in the cross of Christ. The second requires that we embrace crucifixion in ourselves.

The doctrine of repentance, as taught in the Bible, is a call to persons to make a radical turn from a sinful life to a godly life. The repentance called for throughout the Bible is a summons to a personal, absolute, and ultimate unconditional surrender to God as sovereign. The purpose of repentance is to tap into the joy of our union with Christ to weaken our need to do anything contrary to God's heart. It is important to consider how the Gospel affects and transforms the act of repentance.

Luke 15:7, "When the religious crowd of Jesus' day complained that He was spending too much time with the sinners of society, Jesus told them a genuine repentance story. He told the story of the lost sheep. I say unto you, that likewise joy shall be in heaven over one sinner that repenteth, more than over 99 just persons, which need no repentance." Your repentance will deliver you from your sins. So many feel guilty and ashamed about where they are in their walk with God. The enemy continually makes you feel broken beyond repair, hopeless, and beyond forgiveness.

These thoughts leave you feeling forgotten and abandoned by God because you lack the knowledge that He is the same yesterday, today, and forever. He is the faithful One fighting for you!

1 John 1:6 TPT, "If we claim that we share life with him, but keep walking in the realm of darkness, we are fooling ourselves and not living the truth. But if we keep living in the pure light that surrounds him, we share unbroken fellowship with one another, and the blood of Jesus, his son, continually cleanses us from all sin."

I believe that a lack of repentance is debilitating the body of Christ. Most people think they just have to be a good person, but when you compare that knowledge to the commandments given to us by God, we all need a greater understanding to walk in freedom. I will openly admit I had unrepentant sin for the sheer fact I did not know of the sin. While some sin is blatantly obvious, other sin is hidden and must be revealed. When you have never learned God's Word, it leaves you at a terrible disadvantage. I recall learning that pride was a sin that allowed an open door for the enemy to walk right in and attack me.

My pride, rebellion, stubbornness, hatred, and anger hurt me more than I understood. I was just trying to survive, but I was failing miserably according to the Word of God and my lack of knowledge thereof. To say that the crucifixion of my flesh in these areas was excruciating is an understatement. But through His revelation and unfailing love, He never gave up on me and

I learned to persevere. This is the work of the Cross, so you no longer have to stay chained to the sin of your past.

So, lay down your perception of how everything should be, all your ideas of how it will happen, and when it is going to happen. Learn to follow and you will learn to trust God, His goodness, and His desires for your life. You will see victory, for the battle belongs to the Lord. We just have to do our part and allow Him to do His! You will see more clearly.

Prayer: Heavenly Father, I come before you with a humble heart. I recognize that I have sinned in my life. I confess my sins before you and I renounce them. Forgive me for partnering with all sin. I repent for (every sin that comes to mind). I ask you to cleanse me of all unrighteousness and lead me on the path of righteousness for your namesake. In Jesus' name I pray, Amen!

Some sin is generational, passed down to the next generation until someone stands up to the enemy and repents on behalf of their bloodline. Are you called to change your generations?

CHAPTER 6

Out of the Darkness

As I sat there in the darkness, curled up in a corner, feeling broken, rejected, and abandoned. All alone, just as a prisoner locked in a cage. My heart was aching and pounding. The tears would not stop falling. There was no hope found here. I did not know how I would go on from this moment. I found myself in my darkest hour. All I could do was hang my head in disgrace and despair because trauma, sin, and bad choices had brought me here. I kept thinking, who could love such an unworthy sinner like me? From the depth of my being, I cried out... GOD HELP ME!!!

Can you relate to the bitter and lonely place I was in? I had so many against me. I was hated by many and loved by a few.

Micah 7:8 NIV, "Though I sit in darkness, the Lord will be my light." Refers to the deep places of the heart.

Isaiah 42:7 NKJV, "To open blind eyes, to bring out prisoners from the prison, those who sit in the darkness from the prison house."

Suddenly, a tiny ray of light pierced through and penetrated the deep darkness that was surrounding me. *(John 1:1-5 TPT)* As it pierced through and touched my soul, I felt someone there. I turned to look and see who touched me. It was Heaven shining on my soul. I was experiencing the sacred filling of my soul as the light of Jesus filled me. My prayers reached beyond the veil of limitation. There was an exchange beyond the veil at that moment. Darkness no longer existed in that single ray of celestial light. The fire that came with that spirit set my heart ablaze. Instantly, a fire of destiny ignited on the inside of me. It was a beautiful thing. It was a sign of hope in my long, dark night. A moment of revelation broke through my darkness, like the warmth of the sun after a cold, dark night.

I could feel the warmth of my Father's unfailing love, the coming together of being reunited with my Creator. In that majestic moment, there was a coming together of a Father and His daughter. I realized His attention was on me. He knew exactly where I was. I didn't hold back; I reached out. Lifting my hands and heart to receive Him, I was seeking for living water in that dry and thirsty place.

His light immediately healed the wounds of the past. No longer an orphan. He took my lost, lifeless, dying soul and breathed life into it. His presence was life to me. I heard in a far-off distance a soft faint whisper, "My child come closer." Jesus is the way, the truth, and the light. He is calling out your name.

As I moved toward the light, it became brighter. God opened my eyes and I could see more clearly. The darkness lifted, and the fog evaporated. I was no longer alone because an all-consuming fire was burning within me. A tangible light of His presence to grab onto. A living destiny being brought to life. The reality of a faith-filled future, a royal priesthood, and a royal heir. I must fully awaken to live according to my destiny. Now I had the promise of *Psalms 18:28 NLT, "You light a lamp for me. The Lord, my God, lights up my darkness before me."*

My sin disappeared without a trace. I traded it all for who He is! No more fear, no longer thirsty. He asked me to surrender it all and lay it at His feet. I was in awe of His majesty. I bowed my head, overwhelmed by His great love. There is no greater place to be than in the power of His forgiveness, underneath the healing of His wings. He is a merciful Father, full of grace and tender kindness.

I realized at that moment, even in my misery, He was with me. When I was crying in the dark, His love found me. In my wondering and in my running, He wasn't far from me. I wasn't as orphaned and estranged as it seemed in my loneliness. He shined the light of His glory into my darkest hour. Day symbolizes the knowledge of God's will, night/darkness symbolizes the absence of this knowledge. When we move ahead in darkness, is when we stumble.

My life had been extremely hard up to this point because of my choices and the enemy setting out to destroy me. When I accepted Jesus as my Lord and Savior, I had a preconceived idea that everything would be great. I have spoken with many people who have had that same misconception. I had an unrealistic expectation that all my troubles would disappear.

Little did I know the battle would become fiercer. The warfare would intensify. My ship would become more tattered, and my sails more torn. I kept finding myself in these repeated cycles of battles that made me want to give up. Regardless of what is opposing us, our faith is expected to mature.

Learning to be a light even when you are in darkness will teach you to help be a light in someone else's darkness.

Some damage was obvious on the surface, but most was in the unseen areas of my heart and soul.

I had never considered my suffering and broken heart to be a part of God's plan. This made little sense to me. Great sorrow and darkness were all I knew and all I could see. I thought surely this must be because I was the terrible person everyone had claimed me to be.

I experienced so much confusion from the emotions that were raging from the trauma I had experienced. My new awareness caused me to experience mind battles. In looking back, I realized something had dramatically changed, but I was uncertain what changed exactly. My prophetic gifting was thrust into action, and I was immediately more aware of the gift of discernment. I was picking up on the feelings and emotions of other people, along with my own inner turmoil. However, at that time, I was unaware of the spiritual realm and spiritual gifts from God.

It was my brokenness that brought me back to the Lord. My scars have a story to tell. He is raising up the broken out of the ashes. *(Isaiah 42:3; 61:3)* Our journey (process) is a highway to holiness that leads to Jesus. Even with a broken past, you can move on. The Apostle Paul reminds us in *Ephesians 1:4-7 NIV, "For he chose us in him or he chose us in him before the creation of the world to be holy and blameless in his sight. In love he predestined us for adoption to sonship through Jesus Christ, in accordance with his pleasure and will to the praise of his glorious grace, which he has really given us in the One he loves. In him we have redemption through his blood the forgiveness of sins, in accordance with his riches of God."*

Who are the people in darkness? The lost who reject the Word of God and live without the knowledge of Jesus. They lack the understanding of the fullness of God's presence. Also, those who have unfortunately become spiritually unresponsive are blinded by the enemy *(Revelation 3:14-21; 2 Peter 3:17-18)*. Being spiritually blind is the greatest bondage there is. He uses our lack of understanding to keep us in the dark.

The enemy uses our sin to keep us spiritually blind, so we remain spiritually dead. The wounds in our souls could reflect the consequences of the sin in our lives or the sin of past generations. The enemy spiritually blinds us from seeing the truth and from seeing what truly is important for us to gain victory. We are the children of light. Children of darkness move from death to life. It's where dead hearts come alive. We are born with natural sight, but God provides us with spiritual sight. Our sin blinds us from seeing spiritually. It is impossible to see the truth in God's Word *(1 Corinthians 2:14)*.

In *(John 9:25 NIV)*, the man born blind said, "I was blind but now I see." Jesus not only came to heal natural eyes, but to heal the spiritually blind from seeing the truth. The Pharisees who had natural sight asked Jesus (when they doubted who he was) in *(John 9:40-41 NIV)*, *"You mean to tell us that we are all blind? If you would acknowledge your blindness, then your sin would be removed, but now that you claim to see, your sin remains with you!"* Jesus' coming reveals who people are, where they are spiritually and that they are all really in darkness.

In *(John 9:39 NIV)*, Jesus told him, *"For judgment I have come into the world, so that the blind will see and those who see will become blind. He came to give sight to those who are spiritually blind and to show those who think they see they are blind."* In this verse, Jesus is referring to spiritual blindness, spiritual sight, the effects of sin, and the refusal to admit sins. It shocked the Pharisees that Jesus thought they were blind. Jesus countered by saying that it was only blindness (stubbornness, stupidity) that could excuse their behavior.

To those who remained open and recognized how sin had truly blinded them from knowing the truth, he gave spiritual understanding and insight. But He rejected those who had become blind because of complacency and self-satisfaction. The longer this man experienced his new life through Christ, the more confident he became in the One who had healed him. He gained not only physical sight but also spiritual sight as he recognized Jesus first as a prophet in (*John 9:17 NIV*) and then as his Lord and Savior.

If we truly seek Him with all our hearts, we will find out how faithful, merciful, and loving He really is, His character and heart. When you turn to Christ, you see Him differently. The longer you walk with Him, the better you will understand Him. Peter tells us, *"But grow in the grace knowledge of our Lord and savior Jesus Christ (2 Peter 3:18 NIV)."* If you want to know more about Jesus, keep walking with Him. There is a process you must take to get there, but He never leaves, and He never changes.

It is time to get healed and ask God to show you any areas of your heart that need healing. Ask Him to show you any areas that are blocking you from walking in the fullness of Christ. Do not allow your pride or sin to blind you any longer. Pride will keep you from your relationship with Jesus, which will keep you from the breakthrough you need to be healed. Christ is the repairer of the breach for all humankind. His love allows us to overcome all adversity. It is written and we just have to believe it in order to receive it.

He came to set us free. Do not allow the enemy to use those tactics to keep you stuck and use them against you any longer (Christy Johnson, Life Application Study Bible). *Romans 8:11 TPT, "Yes, God raised Jesus to life! And since God's Spirit of resurrection lives in you, He will also raise your dying body to life by the same spirit that breathes life into you."* Resurrection power through redemption will raise the dead. I am redeemed from the curse of sin, sickness, and poverty.

Everything that is a trial or test in your life serves a greater purpose than you know. God is working so many things together for your greater purpose in His kingdom. Your hardship will be the platform of your destiny.

Ephesians 4:21-24 NIV, "when you heard about Christ and were taught in him in accordance with the truth that is in Jesus you were taught with regard to your former way of life to put off your old self which is being corrupted by its deceitful desires, to be made new in the attitude of your minds; and to put on the new self, created to be like God in true righteousness and holiness."

They taught us "to put off the old-self," but we often lack the knowledge of what we need to put it off. Instead, we put off the process, and by doing this, we put off God. This is the first lesson we must learn when walking with God. We must accept the leading of the Holy Spirit and not what any other person says. In this area, listen to what Paul says in *Ephesians 4:30, "And do not grieve the Holy Spirit of God, with whom you were sealed for the day of redemption."* The Holy Spirit has been revealing the areas that have been holding you hostage. Pride and unbelief have kept you from seeing God's truth about your future and His plans for your life. Just remember God works all things for your good. We must keep our focus on Him and not on our past. *Ephesians 5:8-10, "... for once you were in darkness, but now you are light in the Lord. Walk as children of light (for the fruit of the spirit is in all goodness, righteousness, and truth), finding out what is acceptable to the Lord."*

CHAPTER 7

A Warrior Nobody Saw Coming

The following is an account by Amy Scott whom God gave a vision concerning my transition from brokenness to wholeness, and from death to life. She then heard Jesus say: "I have created in you a warrior that nobody will see coming. A warrior that He has kept hidden until this appointed time." There are many hidden warriors that must rise up in this hour and season of time and fight.

There will be one army created to fight the evil forces of our darkest of times. An army of warriors who are unaffected by the enemy. Warriors who know how to fight, who will wage war in the spirit, and intercede in prayer, taking down demonic strongholds of the enemy. The enemy has tried to silence you and keep you in the dark. We battle the forces of darkness through all that we experience. Consider your life and ask yourself who prepared you to wage war?

I have left the 99 in pursuit of YOU (Luke 15)! I am rescuing and delivering you from all that has afflicted you. I am lifting you onto my shoulders! I am taking you back home, where you rightly belong because you are mine. We will rejoice and praise God, our Father, together, and it will be a glorious day. I will set you onto the rock, your firm foundation. I saw you standing in a vast, open area. You stood there looking confused as dust and ash covered you from head to toe. All I could see were your piercing blue eyes looking out in amazement at what was happening.

The dust and the ash were all the things done to you in your life, every betrayal, heartache, and trauma from the past.

The things that were done to you do not define you. They are not the sum of WHO you are!

Old things will pass away like everything else. Now is the time for these things to pass away. There were mistakes and sins, which came down as dust, some light and some heavy. Then there were the things that were done to you, which came down as dark, thick, black ashes, completely covering you, and all I could see was your eyes, blinking, trying to see through all the dirt and ash — opening your spiritual eyes into the spiritual realm. Out of the ashes, hope will arise.

Psalm 19:8 NKJV, "the statutes of the Lord are right, rejoicing the heart: the commandment of the Lord is pure, enlightening the eyes."

Ephesians 1:18 NIV, "I pray that the eyes of your heart may be enlightened, so that you will know what is the hope of His calling, what are the riches of the glory of His inheritance in the Saints."

Take my hand and hold on tight. I am pulling you out of the grave and we will leave it behind, walking away hand-in-hand, my beautiful child! I then saw you look up at the sky. Right over the top of you, a light shined down, and it rained on you. You smiled and cried as the water washed all the dirt and ashes off you. It was so beautiful; you looked so beautiful. It brought tears to my eyes.

I then saw you step out from beneath the sparkling and flowing water and grab a radiant hand, which I believe to be the Father. As you stepped out, you became radiant, smiling and laughing with tears streaming down your face. You then ran over to the rock formation and stood on top of the boulder and started worshipping. I hope you see yourself in this glorious position that Jesus is calling you to as you receive Him. God's power raises us from the dead.

Isaiah 61:3 NIV, "... and provide for those who grieve in Zion- to bestow on them a crown of beauty instead of ashes, the oil of joy instead of mourning, and a garment of praise instead of a spirit of despair, they will be called oaks of righteousness, a planting of the Lord for the display of His splendor."

You are the temple of the Holy Spirit, and you are exactly who God wants to carry His beauty and wear His crown of Glory. You are precisely the right one to display His Glory because He directly hid you for such a time as this. He saved, chose, awakened, and appointed you as a royal priesthood to transform your life into the image of His Son in order for you to carry His presence. He is looking for a yielded vessel to pour out His Glory throughout the earth.

CHAPTER 8

Taking Off The Grave Clothes

Taking off the grave clothes refers to our spiritual awakening, and our resurrection by the miracle working power of Jesus Christ, and as the sons and daughters of the One True God. We were dead men walking until Jesus brought us back to life as those in the shadows emerged, freed from our bonds that enslaved us. Those who suffered injustices had tattered scars from the fierce battle they had been in. Their grave clothes disappeared and with robes of royalty appeared in place of them, and their scars instantly healed.

John Chapter 11 recounts the steps to freedom in removing of grave clothes. It is the story of Mary and Martha and the death of their brother Lazarus. We should note that Jesus loved Mary,

Martha, and Lazarus very much. In brief, Jesus received word that Lazarus was deathly ill. Despite Lazarus' state, Jesus stayed away for more than two days after learning of his sickness.

In the meantime, Lazarus died. When Jesus returned to Bethany, Martha, in her disappointment and grief, blamed Jesus by saying, "If you would have been here, he would not have died." She knew about Jesus healing people.   Jesus declared unto Martha that he was the resurrection and the life and asked her if she believed it. She responded, *"Yes, Lord. I believe that thou art the Christ, the Son of God, which should come into the world (John 11:27 KJV) ."* However, she thought he was referring only to the resurrection when Jesus would come again.

By the time that Jesus had arrived, Lazarus had been dead for four days. It was beyond hope that the spirit of Lazarus would return from the dead. The Jews also commented that since Jesus had healed others, he could have prevented the death of Lazarus. Jesus commanded that the stone sealing the tomb to be removed, but Martha objected, saying that the body was already decaying and stunk. Jesus challenged her by saying that if she would believe, then she would see the glory of God.

As they removed the stone, Jesus prayed aloud that the people might hear and then called forth Lazarus from the grave. The next verse is of great importance. *"And he that was dead came forth, bound hand and foot with graveclothes: and his face was bound about with a napkin. Jesus saith unto them, loose him, and let him go (John 11:44)."* The grave clothes were strips of cheap white linen cloth used to wrap the body with various spices to cover some of the odor of a decaying body. It would be a sight to behold, to see someone alive, coming out of the grave, standing, but still bound hand and foot with grave-clothes. Jesus said, "Loose him, and let him go."

Although Lazarus seemed to be a good person and a close friend to Jesus, he died at a specific time. This is a spiritual picture of humanity. Because of sin, everyone is spiritually dead *(Romans 6:23, 7:9)*. Even though Jesus loves us, He will not prevent the sentence of spiritual death *(Romans 5:12)*. No earthly physician can resurrect one who is spiritually dead *(Matthew 19:25- 26)*. Only through faith in Jesus is there a spiritual resurrection *(John 11:25)*. Jesus is the Way, the Truth, and the Life *(John 14:6)*. Jesus calls people from spiritual death into Life. "Lazarus, come forth" *(Matthew 19:14, 22:14)* (Find Life, Purpose, Joy.) However, after one hears and obeys the call to Life from Jesus, there is still the matter of being bound!

Consider this: the grave clothes still bound Lazarus. He was alive but could go nowhere or do anything. Lazarus could not hear, see, or speak because of the face napkin. In like fashion, many Christians are still bound up. They are spiritually alive, but bound up where they cannot go anywhere or do anything for the Lord. They are bound and cannot hear the voice of Jesus, see spiritual things, or speak or share the Word of God. What grave clothes do you still have on? What is keeping you bound up?

Though Lazarus was no longer dead, he was still wearing a dead man's clothes, not the robes of a victorious believer. Lazarus died so that Jesus' power over death could be demonstrated to the world. The resurrection of Lazarus was an essential display of Jesus' power. The power of the resurrection from the dead, of not only Jesus, but of all disciples, is a critical belief of the Christian faith.

> Jesus has power over life and death; he also had the power to forgive sins because He is the Creator of life. He who is life can surely restore life. Whoever believes in Christ has a spiritual life that death cannot conquer or diminish.

When we realize His power and how wonderful His offer to us really is, how can we help but commit our lives to Him? Here we see many of Jesus' emotions, compassion, indignation, sorrow, even frustration. He often expressed deep emotion and we must never be afraid to reveal our true feelings to Him. He understands them, for He experienced them. Be honest and hide nothing from your Savior because He cares. When Jesus saw the grief, He too wept openly. Perhaps He empathized with their grief. Perhaps He, too, was troubled by their unbelief. In either case, Jesus showed He cares enough for us to weep with us in our sorrow.

What are the grave clothes that keep us bound?

Religion: *"Wherefore if ye be dead with Christ from the rudiments of the world, why, as though living in the world, are ye subject to ordinances, (Touch not; taste not; handle not; Which all are to perish with* *the using;) after the commandments and doctrines of men (Colossians 2:20-22 KJV)?"*

Legalism: *"Therefore let us move beyond the elementary teachings about Christ and be taken forward to maturity, not laying again the foundation of repentance from acts that lead to death, and of faith in God... How much more, then, will the blood of Christ, who through the eternal Spirit offered himself unblemished to God, cleanse our consciences from acts that lead to death, so that we may serve the living God (Hebrews 6:1, 9:14, NIV)."* Dead works are anything we do to obtain or maintain our salvation and will blind believers to God's grace.

Sinful habits: *"Now the works of the flesh are manifest, which are these; adultery, fornication, uncleanness, lasciviousness, idolatry, witchcraft, hatred, variance, emulations, wrath, strife, seditions, heresies, envying's, murders, drunkenness, reveling, and such like: of the which I tell you before, as I have also told you in time past, that they which do such things shall not inherit the kingdom of God (Galatians 5:19-21 NKJV)." "But now ye also put off all these, anger, wrath, malice, blasphemy, filthy communication out of your mouth. Lie not one to another, seeing that ye have put off the old man with his deeds (Colossians 3:8-9 KJV)."*

Failure to understand the exchange at the Cross: *"I have been crucified with Christ and I no longer live, but Christ lives in me. The life I now live in the body, I live by faith in the Son of God, who loved me and gave himself for me (Galatians 2:20, NIV)."* Trying to live the Christian life by our natural abilities rather than the grace of God keeps us in bondage, performing to be accepted and looking for agape love in all the wrong places.

"There hath no temptation taken you, but such as is common to man: but God is faithful, who will not suffer you to be tempted above that ye are able; but will with the temptation also make a way to escape, that ye may bear it (I Corinthians 10:13 KJV) " *"For it is God which worketh in you both to will and to do of his good pleasure (Philippians 2:13 KJV) ."*

Dead and hardened hearts: *Matthew 13:15 KJV, "For this people's heart is waxed gross, and their ears are dull of hearing, and their eyes they have closed; lest at any time they should see with their eyes, and hear with their ears, and should understand with their heart, and should be converted, and I should heal them."*

Mark 4:12, "... so that while seeing, they may see and not perceive, and while hearing, they may hear and not understand, otherwise they might return and be forgiven." Hardened hearts happen when we suffer great disappointment, despair, and many setbacks. Pour out your heart before Him, open your heart and arms to receive Him now, receive the healing your soul desperately longs for. His Mercy is tangible and ever present.

Lukewarm & Complacency: *Revelation 3:16 KJV, "...so then because thou art lukewarm, and neither cold nor hot, I will spit you the out of my mouth."* Lukewarm Christians love to play it safe. They value their security and safety above all else. They are slaves to their fear and will not engage with taking the risk that God has called them to take. They have one foot in the world and one foot in Heaven. God wants your whole heart. Many people have decided to make Jesus their personal Savior but have yet to embrace Him as Lord. Open the door, let Him in.

Many are unaware of their sin and bondages. If you are not sure what keeps you in bondage, pray and ask the Holy Spirit to reveal it. Pray and fast for revelation! There is not anyone who wants you freer than God. The Bible tells us that aside from accepting Jesus Christ, everyone is dead because of their sin. It may be hard to accept this as reality, especially since the unsaved people are clearly walking about, eating, drinking, and doing all the things that living people do. The spiritual reality from God's perspective is that without Christ, we are all as good as dead.

All humanity has sinned and therefore must reap the consequence of sin, which is death. This is a spiritual principle established by God in creation of the universe. When we choose to, intentionally or not, part ways with God, we begin losing our focus and the path that we are to be walking. We are easily distracted from God's plans. Electing to walk the path of potholes instead of His roadway of righteousness, we unwrap ourselves from Him. It is as if we prefer to put the grave clothes back on instead of wearing our garments of grace and holiness.

The choice is quite simple: are we going to offer ourselves slaves to sin or be instruments of righteousness and holiness? Being able to recognize and face that reality can be an issue. The Bible tells us to discipline ourselves to be godly. Temptation often precedes sin, and we can take comfort in knowing that

God has promised that there is no temptation that we cannot overcome.

Knowing there is freedom in Christ:

"We were therefore buried with him through baptism into death in order that, just as Christ was raised from the dead through the glory of the Father, we too may live a new life (Romans 6:4, NIV)."

To put off the old man, we must remove the grave clothes of the sinful nature. It is hard work and requires much time and effort.

FLESH VERSUS SPIRIT

The battle between the two natures rages within us because we now have two opposing forces striving for control over our souls. It is a war being waged between life and death, blessing and cursing, heaven and hell.

As you become more like Christ, your flesh will scream for you to give up. This transformation demands hard work, focus, persistence, and endurance to fulfill God's expectations. Where we once lived according to the ways of the world, with worldly passions and evil thoughts. We are now to live with holiness and righteousness. Yet, our sinful flesh rebels because of it does not want to submit.

Our flesh must come under the authority of the Holy Spirit for us to come in perfect alignment with God. Because we live in such a fast-paced time, it is hard for many to realize the genuine effort it requires. Your flesh wants instant gratification, but does not want to relinquish control. When we do not see things happen in the manner we think or expect, then our flesh wants us to give up. Sometimes, it is difficult to see the forest for the trees.

I remember, after getting saved, how I felt this battle raging between my flesh and spirit, and between my spirit and God. I had such a rebellious soul because of all my past wounds. Out of self-protection, I could not hand it all over to God. I had to have control. I was wrestling with God, thinking, "I know the way. I can handle it. I don't need help." I was too afraid to surrender because I had never learned to trust anyone. My heart had waxed cold. I later learned that I was full of pride and that was an "ouch-a-llujah." When replacing your grave clothes, my sincerest prayer is that the Holy Spirit brings you revelation of the richness of God's love for you and how much He is counting on your freedom to help set others completely FREE!

Psalm 16:11, Eph. 1:5-7 TPT, "...for you bring me a continual revelation of resurrection life, the world to be holy and blameless in his sight. In love he predestined us for adoption to sonship through Jesus Christ, in accordance with his pleasure and will to the praise of his glorious grace, which he has really given us in the One he loves. In him we have redemption through his blood the forgiveness of sins, in accordance with his riches of God's grace, path to the bliss that brings me face to face (your presence) with you."

What has appeared as a far-off sketch to you will eventually become a complete picture. Bright, full of detail and color
beyond comprehension. There are pieces to the puzzle God may
not always reveal to you, but you cannot use your own human
logic to understand it. You must get in the Word of God to learn
the truth. You must learn to trust Him, which means walking in
another level of faith. Maybe you've had a life filled with trauma,
like me, and have little hope or faith.

I went to church in my younger years, but was sitting on the
fence as I got older — one foot in the world and one foot in
church. As your faith grows, God will continue to add parts to
the pieces of your puzzle. They will come together as a part of
His master plan. God will put people in your path to help pull
you out of the darkness and out of the pit.

You are to be a light in the good times and bad times. When
times are dark, the light of God shines brighter to show us the
way from orphan to sonship. We are orphaned because sin cut us
off from God. We were royalty kidnapped by the enemy. Jesus,
our Savior paid the ultimate price to redeem us and restore our
relationship with our Father.

*Romans TPT 8:12-13, "So then, beloved ones, the flesh has no
claims on us at all, and we have no further obligation to live in obedience to it. 13) For when you live controlled by the flesh, you are about
to die. But if the life of the Spirit puts to death the corrupt ways of the
flesh, we then taste his abundant life."*

Our soul should never find peace away from the Lord. God is all we need. We are healed in His presence. No lie you have believed can hold you back or oppress you. God has the final say. His might strengthens us. We are loved by God. No matter how far a person goes into darkness, the light of Jesus will always find them. God can melt even the hardest and coldest of hearts. Do not ever stop standing in the gap for the brokenhearted.

The Holy Spirit is a light that pierces the darkness we find ourselves in. The light that shows us the way. I had a dream. I was driving in darkness, without headlights. It was extremely hard to see. As I drove down the street trying to figure out why there were no lights, a white car appeared from a side road and pulled out in front of me. Suddenly, my car latched onto that car, and it began to pull me as it led the way.

Everything the car did, my car had to follow because we were as one now. When it turned, I had to turn. When it went fast, I went fast. When it went slow, I went slow. When it stopped, I stopped. In this powerful dream, the Lord showed me that we are to follow the supernatural guidance of the Holy Spirit's white car. A gift we receive at salvation. We can hear God's voice when we walk intimately with Him. Be diligent in listening to and honoring the Holy Spirit. He is your lifeline to the Father.

The enemy has blinded us with the wounds in our soul. In this blindness, we cannot see God's true character, His goodness, and that He is a loving father who watches over us. He is faithful and sovereign. Early in my journey with God, He spoke to me and said, "I really need you to discover and know who I am." It was so confusing to me because the word always tells of His mercy and grace. The Holy Spirit will lead you to destiny.

As we draw nigh unto the Lord, He draws nigh unto us. As we get closer to Him, He opens our spiritual eyes so we can see Him and His kingdom more clearly. In our awakening, He will connect us with our destiny. He begins a mighty work in the hearts of those who accept and love Him. *Philippians 1:6 NLT, "And I am certain that God, who began a good work within you, will continue his work until it is finally finished on the day when Christ Jesus returns."* He is revealing, preparing and equipping you for the battle ahead.

Because He has already defeated the enemy, as He lives on the inside of you, everything you need for victory is deep within you.

The power of the Holy Spirit will show you the outcome of the war on your destiny first, which is God's perfect plan for your life. I believe this is to encourage you for the battle ahead. This is where the enemy intensely comes against you with his demonic destruction, with the intent to destroy you (John 10:10). He uses everything in his arsenal to bring you down, steal your faith, rob your joy, and make you give up on God and your destiny.

The enemy launches his strategic plan to prevent you from reaching your calling and destiny. The enemy uses every circumstance in your life, every person he can, to get you into chaos and get you distracted, so he can steer you off course. He creates chaos to make you think he is winning, and that God is mad at you, or does not love you. I have a friend that was in bondage, thinking God hated her. Another stronghold he creates is to make you think, "Oh, I must be doing something so wrong because of these assaults."

He throws up smoke screens and distractions so you cannot see or discern what he is doing to try to defeat you with hopelessness and despair. He will also be constantly working against you with unforgiveness, bitterness, offense, and anger because these spirits create an open door that gives him access to your life and his legal right in the courts to attack you. If he can keep you operating in the flesh instead of the spirit, then he can keep you in bondage. I do not intend to scare anyone but, instead, to educate you about the enemy's tactics and strategies. He targets the saints of God, especially the new ones.

Psalms 43:3 KJV, "O send out thy Light and thy truth: let them lead me; let them bring me unto the holy hill, and to thy tabernacles." I did not have an understanding that Christianity was an excruciating journey to the cross. I did not know that God would have to do such a mighty work in me to clean me up.

Psalms 84:6-7 TPT, "Even when their paths wind through the dark valleys of tears, they dig deep to find a pleasant pool where others find only pain. He gives them a brook of blessing filled from the rain of an outpouring. They grow stronger and stronger with every step forward, and the God of all gods will appear before them in Zion."

FALSE PERCEPTIONS

I did not know the battle would become fiercer. The warfare would intensify, my ship would become more tattered, and my sails would be torn. The wounds of my character assassination were boarded up deep within my soul. I had truly become a battle weary soldier. The anchor holds us in the storms. When we are weary from the battle and when the sea is raging against us we become a broken vessel but through His love, He restores us new for the whole world to see.

I was unaware of the inner healing that I truly needed. I did not understand God or His ways. I was walking blindly because emotionally I was all over the place. My flesh had to die so my spirit could arise. Even when you do not understand where God is taking you, become invested and relentlessly pursue God.

My idea was completely wrong about who the Father really was. I had believed the lies and deceptions of the enemy about God's love for me. The Lord wanted me healed from the past; I had to be emptied, which took time and cooperation.

My example of an earthly father was someone who was absent, leaving me with the feelings of abandonment. My step-dad was always gone, working or drinking. He was passed out most of his time at home or fighting with my mom. While growing up, I thought it was normal for your dad to be absent and withdrawn. This left me as a child feeling lonely, unloved, and unfulfilled. I didn't feel like I had anyone to count on. I did not receive the emotional care, support, and security that are supposed to come with a relationship with your dad. I developed a trust issue from a young age that has followed me all of my life. This issue of trust was how I reflected on my Heavenly Father. I viewed Him as someone I couldn't trust or someone who was unloving and absent. Why else would all of these things happen in my life? I honestly didn't know what a loving father relationship was supposed to look like. I learned about the Father's love and the Father's blessing. It was a hard reality to discover that I had missed out on so much. I had to learn that the Father was trustworthy and I could trust Him. I began to realize that He was good and never changing. I knew the Bible said that He loved all His children, but I doubted that He really loved me. Overcoming these trials and problems rebuilt my faith and trust that He was faithful and "good." We are made in the image of God and He is love. I have been learning about the redeeming power of God's love to restore all that has been stolen from us. While reading the Word of God, I would read the words on the page about the love of God, our Father, but my sin and bad choices left me feeling unworthy and unacceptable to God. My opinion of myself made it impossible to receive His love.

FIGHTING THE WRONG BATTLES

The battles and attacks I had endured left my heart feeling spiritually dead. The Holy Spirit is our lifeline to the Father. The Holy Spirit spoke to me. I recognized and learned to hear and obey the Holy Spirit. We must obey the Holy Spirit and not our flesh. We must walk in the spirit and not the flesh.

Once I truly surrendered and gave my life to the Lord, I said, "Your will Lord, not mine!" He began a healing process through repentance and forgiveness. This process has been an awfully long journey of more than 25 years.

The enemy of our soul is relentlessly warring against us with lies and accusations about ourselves and the ones we love. If he can get us to agree with him by believing his lies, he will continue to accuse and assault us until he can get us to partner with him. He will get us to confess the lies out loud so he can bring about death and destruction in our lives and theirs. There is power in agreement and our confession. We must refuse to help the devil do his job better.

Hebrews 5:8-9 AMPC, "Although He was a Son, He learned [active, special] obedience through what He suffered. V9 and, [His completed experience making Him perfectly [equipped] He became the Author and source of eternal salvation to all those who give heed and obey Him."

He loves us too much to leave us in the mess we have made. He wipes away every stain and transgression. He will use what He deems necessary to get us in His perfect will!

We must break habits and cycles in our lives for God's perfect love to shine forth in us. We should be thankful for the difficult seasons. Amid my deepest pain, and darkest hours, I learned how immediate and tangible His presence could be.

He poured out such tender love and comfort when I needed it the most. Had I not gone through those times, seeking the Father, through His mercy and grace, then I would not have been empowered to overcome the enemy.

I did not understand what He had been trying to do through out my life. I was trying to understand the pain in the process of what I was enduring. It took me some time to realize that I was on a journey with the Lord, and He was doing a mighty work in my life. My viewpoint of God was as a strict disciplinarian. I felt like I was on a tight rope.

I felt as though His love and acceptance were contingent upon my performance of being the best Christian I could be.

I was under so many attacks from the enemy that I could barely keep my head above water. The spiritual warfare was so intense I would try to fight in the best way I knew how, mostly in the flesh and not in the spirit. I kept coming up short and that kept me in a place of despair and discouragement.

The Holy Spirit will lead you out of darkness, but will you follow? Will you do what the Holy Spirit is asking you to do? Sometimes (a lot of times) it will not be something you will want to do or think you should have to do. But remember, the Holy Spirit knows the way and we must surrender. He is faithful; He is always with you when revealing the hidden areas of sin and our flesh that must die. Your flesh dying is a painful process, but it is the only way to move from glory to glory. Even though it hurts, it is the truth that is setting you free. God gives you grace and mercy to sustain you.

The Lord said it is time for those filled with the knowledge of Him to walk as pillars of light. They will walk the earth as giants, for there will be a great shaking everywhere they set their foot. They will bring revelation that shakes the foundation of the earth. All the inhabitants of the land will see proof that God exists. The proof of Him in them will change the thinking of the carnal man. They will never return to their carnal thinking because they will walk with Him. The Bible tells us in *Proverbs 4:18-19 TPT*, *"But the lovers of God walk on the highway of light, and their way shines brighter and brighter until they bring forth the perfect day. But the wicked walk-in thick darkness, like those who travel in fog, and yet do not have a clue why they keep stumbling."*

We can't bow to the things of this world. There is a grace to carry you when you're under fire. The cross bears the burden of the one who set me free. From where I was to where I need to be, He is there with me. In the darkness, He is there with you. The darkness can't stay where He abounds. There is no darkness in Him, only light.

God is creating a movement! He is awakening the sleeping soul. The sons and daughters are awakening. Their dead hearts are being brought to life. All creation is groaning and waiting for God's sons and daughters to realize who they are. There is a resurrection power that lives in us and it is setting us free.

Extra scriptures about walking in darkness:

Psalms 82:5, Ephesians 5:8-9, 11-14, 17, 22; 1 John 1:16, Proverbs 2:13, Lamentations 3:2, Isa 59:9, John 12:35, John 8:12; Isa 47:7, 16, Isaiah 9: 2 NLT

CHAPTER 9

Breaking Up The Old Foundations

In prayer one day, I heard the word "perdition." BibleHub provides the following definitions:

1. "A final state of ruin and punishment, which forms the opposite to salvation....

2. "To be lost" here signifies to have beccme estranged from God,

3. to miss realizing the relations which man normally sustains toward him.

4. It is equivalent to what is theclogically called spiritual death, ruin, and destruction."[11]

---

11. 2022. [online] Available at: <https://biblehub.com/topical/ɔ/perdition.html.> [Accessed 20 March 2022].

The son of perdition is a name given to the antichrist. The Bible tells us those who oppose Christ have the spirit of the "anti christ" denying the Father and the Son (*1 John 2:22*). So, anyone who denies that Jesus Christ is the Messiah or denies that He is the son of God is a liar and a deceiver. We must be on guard for those who profess these things. In Christian tradition, we are told to not trust every spirit but test and see where it comes from (*1 John 4:1*). All that is evil is against God and an abomination of desolation to all who follow it. There is a great rebellion rising against God and all that is good *(2 Thessalonians 2:3)*. People are in danger of going astray because they cannot seem to find their way *(John 14:17)*. In reality, they are just giving up and doing their own things *(Isaiah 53:6)*.

As moral foundations are being destroyed, our society is in danger of collapse. Lawlessness has infiltrated the hearts of many. Gross darkness has covered the earth and is becoming more prevalent than ever. We must open our eyes to see that the devil is at the center of all lies, deception, and false doctrine. Jesus is the only One able to expose, break up, and tear down all darkness, false gods, false religious presumptions, and every demonic structure in your mind, soul, and generations. The enemy will call evil good and all good will be called evil, confusing the hearts of man that do not know the truth in the Word of God *(Isaiah 5:20)*.

In the following scripture, *Psalm 11:3 TPT, "What can the righteous accomplish when truth's pillars are destroyed and law and order collapse?"*

When truth's pillars are destroyed, we see how law and order will collapse. Evil is the opposite of all that is good and righteous. When good stands by and allows evil to take over, that is where we see gross darkness taking over the hearts of man. The decline of holiness and righteousness is the decline of a lost art. So many in this time are bitter, offended, wounded, and broken. We are seeing the great falling away we read about in the Bible. Don't find yourself on the wrong side of all that is godly because you lack the knowledge of the Father and His Son, Jesus Christ *(Acts 3:26).*

Once you are born again, accepting Jesus as your Lord and Savior, the Holy Spirit enters your life and begins to *".... tear down walls that separate us (Ephesians 2:14)."* The Holy Spirit breaks up the old foundations of the world and your past as you have known them. He will begin to separate us from the bondage that has kept us out of relationship with God the Father. As we awaken and surrender, we become sanctified, holy, and devoted to God. God puts us into our rightful place of inheritance as His sons and daughters.

Jesus in you transforms your old life from sin and death to a new life of relationship, love, healing, deliverance, and obedience to Jesus. Your desires change from craving sin to craving the presence and power of God. Darkness shatters when it collides with Jesus.

Jeremiah 23:29, "Is not my word like fire, declares the Lord, and like a hammer that breaks the rock in pieces."

You will experience a new found spiritual freedom as the past false religious mindsets and traditions diminish. Jesus is creating a greater anointing and authority in you for His Glory. He tears down the false identity the enemy has created on the earth and in our hearts.

We have all authority over the enemy. As Jesus restores God's covenant in our hearts and generations, we learn and grow in exactly what that means. This will take great humility on your part. We must lay all pride at the altar. Pride and surrender are at odds with each other. Pride will tell you that you are fine and nothing needs to change. However, the Holy Spirit is telling you the truth about your situations. Go low in humility in order to soar higher in the things of God. Let go of every encumbrance the enemy has attached to your life. Every time you have tried to take off these, strings of attachment have pulled you back and kept you stuck. In your humility, the Lord will cut the strings that hold you back.

The breaking up of these false foundations is a very shaky and emotionally unsettling time. Sin has infiltrated into our hearts and lives through the false beliefs of the enemy. All darkness must be broken and torn down in order to restore us to covenant with God.

Until we meet Jesus, sin is all we known. By the world's standards, most people are decent people. That's why it is a spiritually challenging process. We do not understand God or His ways. At least I didn't. God revealed the shifting sand of my foundation. It was a life built on a foundation of chaos instead of peace.

I didn't have a clue or understand all that would have to change. My world was literally turned upside down. Although it was complete chaos, I had become very familiar with how to operate and survive there. The Word says, *'My people perish because of a lack of knowledge (Hosea 4:6)."* It's hard to find the truth from the pulpit these days, but the truth brings us freedom. Thankfully, all truth is in the Word of God. Change has to be inevitable if you want a godly life of peace and abundance. We cannot expect our life to change and be different if we don't make it different. God is revealing to us that this process can take an awfully long time. Although, it truly depends upon your submission and cooperation with the Holy Spirit. When the breaking up begins, the healing process of who you were originally created to be comes to the light and becomes more and more apparent over time.

Now, what is a spiritual foundation? The underlying principle refers to the character of a person. An individual with great character is one who is secure in their identity in Christ and chooses to affect the world instead of being affected by the world. Godly character is the cornerstone of a person's structure. Our righteousness is the foundation that gives power to our confession. Jesus is the Chief Cornerstone, our noble example of strength and stability. Our goal on the Earth should be that when people look at us all they see is Jesus.

Matthew 7:24-27 NIV, "Therefore, everyone who hears these words of mine and puts them into practice is like a wise man who built his house on the rock. The rain came down, the streams rose, and the winds blew and beat against that house; yet it did not fall, because it had its foundation on the rock. But everyone who hears these words of mine and does not put them into practice is like a foolish man who built his house on sand. The rains came down, the streams rose, and the winds blew and beat against."

The condition of your foundation matters. What lies and foundational errors are ensnaring you and your bloodline?

We need to recognize what we have fallen prey to such as fear, addiction, sexual perversion, incest, poverty, sickness, disease, mental health issues, and premature death. Are you caught in the enemy's snare of demonic structures containing anger, hatred, offense, bitterness, betrayal, victim mindset, death, suicide, rebellion, destruction, stubbornness, witchcraft, and self-pity? The Lord is exposing the attributes of Jezebel by tearing down the altars and foundations of witchcraft that have crept into our lives. Jezebel brought in the false god of Baal, and it spread throughout the land and demanded everyone to worship it. It took over the lives of most. Queen Jezebel was the wife of King Ahab who ruled the Kingdom of Israel. Their story is found in the Bible in King 1 and 2. Do you know what is drawing you? What are you being drawn to? This will help you determine how to demolish the demonic structures in your bloodline. Here is a list of a few:

- Rebellion
- manipulation
- murder
- control
- dominating
- intimidation
- invokes fear
- stress and anxiety
- pride
- selfishness
- cunning
- subtle
- seductive
- plant seeds of discord
- creates division
- religious
- own agenda
- uses others for personal gain
- lies
- deceives
- attacks anointed
- camouflages as godly
- loyal until you disagree with them.

This demonic spirit will shut down your prophetic voice and gift if you do not stand up to it and use your authority. I stifled my gift because I cowered down and isolated myself from people and the church. I would allow people and their opinions and perception to cause me to be so emotionally unstable.

I came from an exceptionally large family on my mother's side with 16 children, eight boys and eight girls. My mother was the second to the youngest. As I reflect on my family's sin cycles, their impoverished state stands out. I can only imagine how challenging a family that size must have been. The spiritual, mental, and physical decline became more apparent as the enemy took complete advantage of so many. In their weakened and impoverished state, the enemy took complete advantage of those curses. With force and cruelty, the enemy reigned over them for several generations. I hope to reveal to you some of these cycles and teach you how to break them. To learn how to spiritually fight the demonic forces of darkness coming against you and your future generations.

I am not trying to say that some of my family members are not God-fearing people who loved God. It wasn't discussed much. My grandmother was a churchgoing woman who loved God with all her heart. I cannot imagine how hard life had to be for her. I am just saying there were curses affecting the lives of so many who were completely unaware of the enemy that was opposing and depressing them.

Yes, I agree this really stinks because most people are not even aware of these curses, but it is God's law. There are legal contracts in Heaven about you that need to be broken. The enemy accuses us day and night before God in Heaven with generational sin (*Revelation 12:9-11*). In reading this, do not get caught up in fear because God's plans trump the enemy's plots. God is the giver of all life. He sustains our life; therefore, it is important to know who He is.

I am sharing my journey with you so you can track your journey with God and where He is planning to take you. I want to help you understand the process that took years for me to understand. I want to open your eyes to the enemy who trespasses into your life to mess that plan up. I think too many families are keeping things swept under the rug, giving the enemy a tighter grip on their lives and the demise of the bloodline.

God has a great plan. I am trying to bring revelation of the enemy's activities behind the scenes. When you are but a child, the enemy works relentlessly against God's plan for your life. He plots a series of events to bring destruction and death into your life. This is the reality of my life. Upon conception, the enemy began fulfilling those generational curses. Sin will empower those generational curses until someone stands in the gap and changes that bloodline back to God.

Are you called to be a history changer? I believe God is calling forth His curse breakers. I believe the Father is looking throughout the earth for those willing to stand in the gap. As an heir and joint heir to Christ Jesus, it is your inheritance. Most Christians are not even aware they have an inheritance from the Kingdom of God. This is where the breaches in the wall developed. My great-grandfather was a preacher walking closely with God. He saved many souls under his ministry. I believe he tried to keep his entire family walking with the Lord. The next generation is where the falling away began. Everything I have heard and read leads me to believe this. My grandfather abandoned his family when my mom was only three years old. This left her with abandonment and rejection issues.

This rejection and abandonment left her feeling orphaned. Even though she was unaware, she was bitter, angry, and rebellious, which was passed along to me. Growing up without knowing my biological father was heartbreaking. I struggled with this most of my life. This left me wondering and guessing my whole life, who was my dad? Where he was? My intentions are not to hurt anyone with this chapter, but sometimes the truth needs to be told, so restoration can come forth. Every hidden sin in the dark is a weapon the enemy can use against you and torment you with it day and night *(See Psalm 25:4-10)*.

We must partner with the Holy Spirit and trust this restructuring process *(Isaiah 43:3)*. The Holy Spirit is a constant eternally divine presence in a believer's life. To receive the Holy Spirit, you must be born again, apart from a physical birth, and experience a spiritual birth. The Holy Spirit will take up residence in the life of the new believer to bring him or her to spiritual maturity.

The book of Acts gives a very plain account of the promised Holy Spirit *(Acts 2)*. Jesus tells us, *"When the Helper comes, whom I will send to you from the Father, that is the Spirit of truth who proceeds from the Father, He will testify about Me (John 15:26, NASB95)."* It is important that we learn to recognize and follow the leading of the Holy Spirit. If we don't, we will fall into the spirit of error, which is the opposite of the Spirit of Truth. The Father has delivered us from death and hell and will rebuild and create a new firm foundation within us and restore us back to covenant with Him. He will align us with Heaven.

If we will stay close to Him and keep following the wind of His spirit, He will guide us in all truth. He will take us higher and higher. Once and for all, you will fly high above the restraints of the enemy, those strings that are attached to you and keeping you from all that He has for you. You will soar far above where the enemy can go or where he can operate. The Holy Spirit is leading you to a resurrected life of spiritual truths as you surrender your will. Your flesh tries to stay in control with its prideful and lofty ideas. I quarreled with my Maker because my flesh had been in control for so long. I had a very hard time submitting and surrendering.

Therefore, it is so important to partner with the Holy Spirit, so you can learn how to overcome. It is important to understand that every child of God has their own personal war to fight. It only takes one generation to move away from God *(Judges 2:10)*. It only takes one person to turn a bloodline back to God. Curses and sin keep us from being in covenant with God. God did not intend for us to remain independent from Him. We are His covenant people.

What is God's Covenant? It is a legal contract, oath, pledge, vow, pact, or treaty. In the Bible, an agreement exists between God and his people. God makes promises to His people requiring certain conduct from them. The covenant agreement is the way the Bible portrays the relationship between God and His people and (to a lesser extent) all humanity. Many scholars debate the actual number of covenants, but the Bible mentions five: Noah, Abraham, Israel, David, and Messianic (Jesus).[12]

The first covenant begins with Noah (The Rainbow) when God promises to never flood the earth again *(Genesis 9:1-17)*. The covenant of redemption and grace that governs the Bible begins with Abraham *(Genesis 12-17)*. This is where the pattern of the covenant became firmly established. Right at the outset, in the story of the call of Abraham, the most obvious rhetorical pattern is the language. God continues with Israel in Exodus, King David *(2 Samuel 7:8-17)*, and finally with Jesus (*Matthew 26:26-35)*.

There is a proper order set by God in each person's life. Walking in that proper alignment is essential for all our relationships in life. There is a healthy Christ-centered way where the Spirit of God flows throughout our relationships. The fall of Adam and Eve hurt our walking in God's order. Eating from the tree of knowledge of good and evil made them independent from God and that sentence of death passed on to the whole human race. Part of us does not want to submit to God, and part of our rebellious state doesn't want to submit to others.

Our soul came under the charge of Satan. We have become the center of our own world, making my own choices and doing our own thing. Our independence puts us out of God's alignment and protection. Christ is the head of every man. He is God's substitute for death. He broke our bondage link to Satan.

---

12. BibleProject. 2022. Covenants: The Backbone of the Bible | BibleProject™. [online] Available at: <Https://Bibleproject.com/Blog/Covenants-The-Backbone-Bible> [Accessed 20 March 2022].

Now we are again free to choose. We must choose obedience and trust in God in order to be in His perfect will.

We depend on God. Our spirit totally submitted to God and His authority in our life covers us with God's protection. We die to self and yield to God. God did not design us to make it on our own. If a man is not under Christ's covering, he will be unprotected from the attacks of the enemy. There are benefits to walking in alignment. The blood of Jesus Christ covers us and works as a shield for our whole being when our Spirit is on top. Attacks from the enemy cannot penetrate the protection of the blood. The blood of Jesus is a powerful weapon against the enemy. The cleansing provided by the blood keeps our minds and emotions protected *(Isaiah 32:17).*

When our spirit is governed by the Holy Spirit, He will speak directly to our spirit. Our soul is quiet and at rest in submission to our spirit. We can hear His still small voice and understand what He is saying to us. As we agree with God's Word, our lives come back into alignment with our spirits, souls, and bodies operating in their proper roles is pleasing to God. Then we can walk as God intended us to walk straight, upright, in a posture of wisdom and strength. As I have grown spiritually after becoming a new creation in Christ led by the Holy Spirit, my spirit has influenced my soul more and more. I receive wholeness, protection, grace, peace, and anointing. My identity in Christ is the greatest truth about who I am and the destiny He has for me. I learn what God Himself has to say about me and not man. There is no greater power than believing and confessing the truth about myself.

I am no longer my sin; my sin no longer defines me. Knowing this, combined with humility and repentance, closes the hidden places of the enemy in my life. In God, there are many areas of alignment, both personal alignment and relational alignment. When we walk in alignment, the peace and protection of the Lord will be upon our lives. As your whole family comes into alignment, they will see the glory of God. There will be stability and growth happening in our lives, and we will hear the voice of the Lord.

PROCLAMATION OF WALKING IN ALIGNMENT:

I am a spirit. The Holy Spirit connects to my spirit. My spirit is like Jesus' spirit! I choose God's will for me and submit myself to Him. I reject the sins and works of the flesh. I reject (these things I struggle with) _____. I clothe myself with the garments of salvation and the robe of righteousness. Lord, I invite you to search and cleanse the deepest parts of me. I renounce every hidden thing of darkness in my life. I put on the new nature. I choose to walk in the spirit. I choose the fruit of the spirit. I walk in the authority, love, and power of God. *The Lord is my Shepherd, and He supplies all of my needs (Psalm 23:1)*. I trust Him with my life and all my issues. I am all that the Word says I am. I have all that the Word says I have. I can do all that the Word says that I can do. I am strong in the Lord and in the power of His might *(Ephesians 6:10)*. I will walk in the path the Lord has destined for me, and I will fulfill the calling that He has for me. I am a joy to Him, and He is pleased with me. Giving Him pleasure is my highest priority!

To consecrate is to release to God and place under His control. It also means to set aside for the Lord. Lastly it means to yield, surrender, and commit to the Lord. When we commit an area, a situation or a person to the Lord, we are trusting the outcome to the hands of who He is. God is able and willing to take care of them. We must not worry, fear, or hold unto unforgiveness or other negative emotions because it causes us to think the worst. Do not give Satan any words that allow him control in your life. Allow your words and emotions to be transformed by saying, "Lord, I believe you and I praise you."

We must consecrate the following specific areas to the Lord:
1. **material possessions:** money, boats, cars, house, jewelry, sports;
2. **relationships:** job, spouse, parents, children, boss, co-workers, in-laws, enemies; and
3. **self:** sin, talents, goals, ambitions, pleasures, pride, ego, opinions, rights, and fears.

Submission in these areas to Jesus is the only way to live freely. God didn't create us to be separated from Him. All of us are controlled by either God or Satan. Any area consistently not consecrated will rise to the place of dominion and control in our lives. It will pull us out of alignment and provide a lodging place for the enemy.

There was a deep emptying of self in Peter's life through his failures. Because there was less of Peter, there was more room for Jesus. Peter preached a sermon in *Acts 2:14*. How many people received Christ because Peter trusted God and not himself? Weakness and inadequacy of self is a big aspect of our consecration to God. Everything that we consecrate to God will fall under the blessing of God and His protection. This allows your spirit man to be free in the place of dominion.

Consecration sets the stage for us to be free from any demonic influence or control. As we seek God in His Word, that Word works inside of us, exposing to us self, wrong motives, wrong thinking, selfishness, and impurities. These things come out of our soul and not our spirit. The greater our spirit and soul are separated, the more clearly we will distinguish between what is of us, the soul and what is of God, and our spirit. This will make it easier to hear from God clearly. It is at the very heart of being sanctified, so that we can stop walking after our own wisdom and impulses and remain in alignment with God.

Let us seek God humbly so that He can work in us in ways that our spirits and souls would become separated and we could walk in greater and greater obedience to the Lord. Consecration is a change in our hearts. Victory comes when we repent and then turn from sin. Meekness is submitting our flesh to God in the difficult thing and not allowing ourselves to rise to defend and protect ourselves. Remember, pride fights back in the flesh against that which opposes your flesh.

The fruit of the spirit is meekness. Meekness shuts down self. It is like the on-off switch for self. Give meekness an inch and it will give you a mile. Meekness turns around the negativity of others. Patience and meekness are a good team. You don't assimilate the hurt. The more we clear us out of the way, the more we can take hold of God. He took all of me on the cross and gave me all of who He is. We must abide in His Word, consecrate all that we have to Him, and pick up our cross daily. This enables us to be mended, healed, and set free and progressively brought more and more into the image of Christ. There is a difference between repenting of a sin and pulling down the stronghold of a sin that has taken root. The first involves faith in the cross of Christ. The second requires that we embrace crucifixion in ourselves. So, we are changed from the old man to the image of Christ Jesus.

CHAPTER 10

Order from Chaos

It all begins with salvation. How to accept Jesus? First, believe in the salvation of Christ. *"For God so loved the world that he gave his one and only Son, that whoever believes in him shall not perish but have eternal life (John 3:16, NIV)."* Second, confess your sins before God. *"If you declare with your mouth, 'Jesus is Lord,' and believe in your heart that God raised him from the dead, you will be saved (Romans 10:9, NIV)."*

In the Hebrew language, Jesus means salvation. The Son of Man's purpose for coming into the world is to seek and save the lost *(Luke 19:10)*. Salvation belongs to God alone. Peter's certainty of this relation between "Jesus Christ of Nazareth, whom you crucified" and the God "who raised him from the dead" moves him to the exclusive confession that salvation belongs only to the name of Jesus Christ *(See Acts 4:10-12)*.

Jesus taught that salvation is vital to advancing the Kingdom of God. Salvation belongs to God, for the Kingdom signifies a sphere of reality in which God reigns sovereign. Salvation belongs to those who follow Jesus, the bringer, and embodiment of God's Kingdom. Salvation is the mystery of God that is now revealed, and a plan conceived before the foundations of the world. Salvation has been described in various ways: a light for revelation to the gentiles, a transition from death to life, a message especially for sinners, a gift of grace through faith, not dead works, that for which the whole creation groans, the revelation of God's righteousness to faith and for faith, the justification that comes through faith, reconciliation, and redemption.

In response to Nicodemus' question, *John 3* offers that salvation is a spiritual birth from above without which one cannot enter the Kingdom of God *(John 3:1-11)*. Salvation means death to and freedom from sin, a new perspective that transcends the human point of view and participation in a new creation. Peace with God, life as an adopted child of God, baptism into Christ's death, and the reception of the Holy Spirit.

Salvation encompasses both the physical and spiritual dimensions of life, having relevance for the whole person. The forgiveness of sins and physical healing frequently coexist, as in the healing of the paralytic *(Mark 2: 1-12)*. Other healings that are done in Jesus' name call attention to the intimate connection among spirit, mind, and body. What Jesus did in our name, he also did in our place, giving his life as the ransom for many. And if Christ shows his love by dying when we are all sinners,

how much more will his life change us? So critical is the resurrection to your future hope of salvation, ".... that if Christ has
not been raised, your faith is futile; you are still in your sins."*(1
Corinthians 15:15-19)*

"Salvation is personal repentance and faith; the cross is
the power of God for those who are being saved *(Romans 1:16)*.
Paul tells his readers to work out their salvation with fear and
trembling *(Philippians 2:12)*. And there is yet a salvation that
lies waiting to be revealed in the last time, every redemption
for which we groan inwardly *(Romans 8:23)*. For Paul, the past
dimension of salvation is conceived as justification, redemption,
and reconciliation, while it presents dimension, it is to be de-
picted in terms of the spirit sanctifying work. The future dimension is glorification, the culmination of the saving process
whereas believers will experience Christ present and the new
and resurrected bodies that are no longer burdened with the
vestige of sin."[13]

Upon receiving Jesus Christ as my Lord and Savior, I began
attending church regularly. I experienced another encounter
with the Holy Spirit. He was refreshing, and His presence awakened my spirit. I honestly felt like I was home, exactly where I
was supposed to be. This feeling of the Lord's presence is amazing and invigorating. I grew up attending the Methodist church,
which is nothing like a nondenominational church where the
Spirit of God can freely flow. It was nice to gain a new church
family because at this point in my life, I felt all alone.

13. biblestudytools.com. 2022. Salvation - Biblical Meaning and Definition in Christianity. [online] Available at: <https://www.biblestudytools.com/dictionary/salvation/>
[Accessed 20 March 2022].

As I became acquainted with my new church and spiritual family, I became more aware of the supernatural presence of God, the spiritual realm, and spiritual gifts. So many things made sense to me, and yet many things overwhelmed me. I was so thankful to God because He knew just what I needed. He planted me where I needed to be to get deeply rooted in the Word of God and the gifts of the Holy Spirit. It created such a hunger and thirst in my spirit, I could not get enough. I attended church every time the doors opened. I dug into the Holy Scriptures; it was amazing how much knowledge I gained.

I know this might sound a little crazy, but for the first time I realized that all the Christian music was about God and all the secular music was about the flesh and the worldly ways. My eyes were open to the reality that there was so much more to life than I had experienced. I was desperate for my life to change and hopeful for a normalcy that I has seen other people experience. I noticed that the only people who had peace were the people who served God and had accepted Jesus as their Lord and Savior. I wanted to experience that love and peace in my heart and my relationships.

I deeply wanted that for my husband and children. I knew the cross was a beautiful exchange for eternity, but because of being so naïve and lacking knowledge and wisdom in the ways of God, I thought I would instantly exchange all the bad and replace it with everything Jesus died to give me. I thought salvation was an instant exchange. It was, but not the way I was thinking. I was a daughter of the Kingdom of God. A royal priest with an inheritance taken from glory to glory, but I did not know of that fact. I did not know it would be a journey. It was a long process that would be 30 years in the making. It is vital to stay committed to the process.

It has been a race that I have run and run for what seems like an eternity. I was a weary soldier. Going through dark storms that never seemed to end. I continued to get beaten by life's circumstances. Everything had been very disheartening and disappointing when I learned how broken and lost I really was. I was a complete mess, and it has taken many years of partnering with the Holy Spirit to get set free from the Jezebel Spirit and walk in true Godly authority and power to overcome the evil of this hour in history. Your entire existence on the Earth is to be filled with God's glory and carry it throughout the Earth. You are a chosen one put on the earth to be brought forth in God's perfect timing. Unbeknownst to me, I was being trained, and equipped to be a valiant warrior in the army of the Lord for the end time battle. A battle-ready warrior forged in the fire. One who has persevered through every attack of the enemy sent to break me and stop me.

There has been strategic warfare God allowed to bring me into my full inheritance as a daughter of the King. You must be aware and learn your true identity in Christ because you are stronger than you think, stronger than what the enemy has made you believe. You are ready for the battle ahead, so don't doubt Him who has already overcome the enemy you are facing because He has instilled mighty weapons in you, weapons that are mighty to the pulling down of strongholds and principalities.

You will never stop learning and growing in the things of God unless you give up or just quit. Trust me when I say that the enemy is relentlessly after your destiny, faith, and future.

It's impossible to fight a full-time devil as a part time Christian. My entire purpose of sharing my journey with you is to encourage you to keep fighting, keep going, and charge on. Through a series of prophetic encounters, the Lord brought to light the mandate and assignment that He had for me in my future destiny. We walk and war in His strength. This will require humility and dependence on God. I want you to understand what I was completely unaware of and had no clue about what was happening in the natural, physical, or supernatural realm. In my personal experience, God showed me the plans and purposes He had for my life.

Through prophetic words and dreams, God laid out those plans. He showed me the end of the journey and what I would walk in. It makes you very excited to see how God plans to use you, but unfortunately our zeal and pride cause us to get puffed up about what His plans are and how great they are. Our pride and worldly ways have to be worked out of us and that happens by your flesh dying to self. I now believe He does this so you can have something to keep fighting for when you are in the toughest battles, and you feel you cannot go on. When you are in the wilderness for a long time, there are so many unanswered questions.

I kept saying, "What is the point?" I am a matter-of-fact kind of person and I wanted to understand with my natural mind. I later learned that it is a process that unfolds as the puzzle pieces come together one by one. There is a set timing that is beautiful in its time that brings forth the light of your destiny and gifting. Along this journey with the Lord, you will grow in your faith and your relationships will deepen. You will uncover His undying love for you personally. He will show you He has nothing but good intentions and plans for you, plans to prosper you (*Jeremiah 29:11*). He will dispel every lie the enemy has been speaking into your ear about who you are not. You will see yourself through the Father's eyes. You will see your life and calling differently.

I will explain how we experience the end first, so when we are in the trenches of the battle, in the barren place, or the wilderness, we can hope for our prophetic promises. There will be times when you have to fight and war for your promises to come to fulfillment when the enemy is trying to shut you down.

God's intention and desire is to have His people use the gifts of the Holy Spirit and the gift of prophecy. Prophetic ministry brings God's perspective, releases calling and vision, and undermines the enemy by igniting faith and hope, thus giving inner strength to fight on and to bring breakthrough. An important role of the prophetic ministry for today is revealed in scripture as we read *Ephesians 4:13, "Till we all come to the unity of the faith and of the knowledge of the son of God, to a perfect man, to the measure of the stature of the fullness of Christ."*

The objective of the prophetic ministry is not only to prophesy, but to reach the full maturity in Jesus, our Lord. Fullness happens when we commune with God (intimate knowledge) and community (relational connection) with others. If the stated goal of God is to use the prophetic ministry to bring a mature expression of Jesus on the earth, then it makes sense that for this to happen, we need mature prophetic ministers to arise. For us to be mature in the prophetic, our personal relationship with God and inter-relationships with others must be a priority.[14]

I attended my first woman's retreat for the first time. I really did not know what to expect, but I came with a great expectancy of being touched and changed by God. He did not disappoint me. I want to share a timeline with you to help you understand the process He takes you through. I want to show you how God shows you the end of your journey as you begin. I believe this keeps you running the race set before you. You hunger and thirst for that result of God's glory to help get you through the really tough battles.

The first night, the Pastor announced we would receive a new name by the end of the weekend. We needed to be asking and seeking God for that name. She said God would reveal it to us. Because I knew nothing of the prophetic, I had no clue how God would do this. That night before I fell asleep, I envisioned a large flowing waterfall. I thought, "Wow. I wonder what that means?"

The next day, I got the word "Glory." It just popped into my thoughts. In searching for what it meant, I learned "glory" is

---

14. Buttner, Len. "Post Author:Len Buttner." Eagle Ascend. Accessed May 11, 2022. https://eagleascend.com/distinctive-kinds-of-prophetic-utterances/.

defined as "the manifestation of God's presence."[15] God is most glorified in us when we are most satisfied in Him.

That night I got the scripture, *"Arise, shine; for your light has come, and the glory of the LORD has risen upon you. "For behold, darkness will cover the earth And deep darkness the peoples; But the LORD will rise upon you And His glory will appear upon you (Isaiah 60:1–2, NASB95)."*

And Jesus' declaration to Martha and Mary at the tomb of Lazarus, *"Jesus said to her, "Did I not say to you that if you believe, you will see the glory of God (John 11:40, NASB95)?""*

On the last day of the retreat, we told everyone the name we received from the Lord. I felt led to share the name "Glory." The Lord said that he was going to pour out his Glory through me like a mighty waterfall. That was amazing to me. I did not even know if what I received was from the Lord or if it was biblical truth. But many years later, I learned that I would be a Glory Carrier and host the presence of the Lord. Many years later, that name was confirmed, and *(Isaiah 60:1-2)* has been a lifelong scripture for me. A promise that I have held onto throughout the years of relentless attacks from the enemy.

At the same retreat, while I was giving my testimony, a lady there had a vision of me. She said that she had seen me in a baby carriage. As she moved closer to the carriage, I suddenly got out of the carriage an older and more mature person. I was holding a machete and started wielding it with great skill and

15. En.wikipedia.org. 2022. Glory (religion) - Wikipedia. [online] Available at: <https://en.wikipedia.org/wiki/Glory_(religion)> [Accessed 20 March 2022].

accuracy. She told me the Lord told her, I was going to be looked at by many in the Body of Christ as a baby, but I would suddenly come on the scene and surprise them all with the wisdom and knowledge I had received from the Lord and would accurately share and help many people who were struggling. I also learned from this vision that it was going to take a while to get where I was going, but soon realized that things were going to happen in God's timing, and I held onto that memory whenever I would get discouraged about how long it was taking.

Since that conference, God has affirmed His prophetic calling upon my life. A prophet affirmed by divine calling as an evangelist, meaning, "... a person who seeks to convert others to the Christian Faith, especially by public preaching."[16] And again, a prophet (the first time I met him) prophesied over me saying, "God did not make these hands for shaving (I'm a hairdresser and he did not know that). He made these hands for saving. I see you saving thousands upon thousands of people. You have a strong anointing and God is taking you to the nations."

The same preacher came again about a year later. This time, he preached on the fire of God. I had no knowledge or understanding of what that was. It was really getting hot in there, is all I know. He called for an altar call and I started walking to the front and He lunged forward and said FIRE and just like that, I was on the floor and could not get up. I was freaking out because he never even touched me. I was at least 5 feet away from him. And I thought, "Dang, if God can knock you down like that, we really are but dust." I honestly knew from that encounter that

16. Price, P., 2006. The prophet's dictionary. New Kensington, Pa.: Whitaker House.

God was real. The preacher came and prayed for me and said, "You have a fire in your mouth, fire in your hands, you are a deliverer of fire." The fire of God is an intense heat that heats you up all over your body. The fire burns up all works of darkness. There is healing and deliverance in the fire of God (Jeremiah 20:8-9). I remember receiving a word of knowledge from the woman's pastor about my anointing, how it was like a fire burning everything in my path. It was burning the enemy, burning others, and it was burning me.

I remember thinking, "What is an anointing?" You may even wonder that same thing. It must be about my mouth because my mouth gets me into trouble all the time. The anointing is a "sacramental rite whereby the acts or effects of being chosen for delegated position or purpose are signified by pouring or smearing oil upon a person elevated to an office."

Scriptures on the fire of God:

Psalm 140:10, "Release the spirit of fire to burn up the works of darkness."

Malachi 3:2, "Purify my life with your fire."

Jeremiah 23:29, "Let your word be preached with fire, is not my word like fire? Says the Lord. 'And like a hammer that breaks the rock to pieces?'"

Hebrews 1:7, "Who makes His angel spirits and His ministers a flame of fire.

Make me a minister of fire."

Let your fire be on my tongue to preach and prophesy. I receive tongues of fire.

Let your fire be in my hands to heal the sick and cast out devils.

Let your fire burn in my eyes, my heart, my belly, my mouth, and my feet.

The next prophetic encounter that I experienced was at a home prayer meeting. When I arrived, I only knew one person there. A lady whom I had known for a long time because I did her hair. Prayer meetings were very new to me, but I was hungry and thirsty for more of God and His presence. Everyone stood in a circle and prayed as we listened to worship music.

The presence of the Lord overwhelmed me. There is so much peace and healing in His presence. I was desperately in need of His peace in my chaotic state.

They were praying in the spirit; a heavenly language. I was not familiar with what that was, but I could feel the atmosphere changing and shifting. I had never experienced that before, but it was a wonderful feeling. A woman there started praying for people. When she got to me, she laid her hands on me and I was on the floor, "slain in the spirit," which was also a first for me. Slain in the spirit is a term used by the Charismatic Christian to describe the individual being overcome by the power of the Holy Spirit. Believers attribute this behavior to falling under the power and presence of God.[17] There was a heavy weight on me, and I couldn't get up, so I just laid in the presence of the Lord.

When the meeting was ending, the lady that prayed for everyone asked the other ladies there if anyone had any revelation about what happened to me. I was thinking, "That would be wonderful!" One lady said that she had seen in the spirit the mantle of Elijah falling from Heaven on me. I had no clue what that was or what it meant. It honestly took years for me to understand the magnitude of what had happened that day. The weight I had experienced that day was the "Kabod Glory" of the Lord.

The Bible speaks of God's glory as an extension of God's being. When the Lord walked past Moses, God's glory touched

17. "Slain In The Spirit." Wikipedia. Wikimedia Foundation, February 2, 2022. https://en.wikipedia.org/wiki/Slain_in_the_Spirit

him *(Exodus 33:12-33)*. The glory of the Lord filled the Temple courts with His presence *(1 Kings 8:10-11)* blinding the worshippers with smoke. When the angels appeared before the shepherds, "And an angel of the Lord suddenly stood before them, and the glory of the Lord shone around them; and they were terribly frightened *(Luke 2:9, NASB95)*. What I felt that night, laying there on the floor was "the full presence of the Lord."[18]

It is a way of our witnessing His beauty and radiance. This is when I began my research on the mantle of Elijah.

Who was Elijah? Elijah means "Jehovah is my strength," or "Yahweh is my God." Elijah was a bold and fearless prophet of God who was direct and to the point. Elijah was a prophet that stood for God despite the enormous obstacles he endured. He was a human being just like you and me. He had hopes, dreams, weaknesses, and shortcomings. Despite the powerful moments in his life when he performed dramatic miracles, he still struggled with fear, doubt, and depression.

Despite his shortcomings, Elijah was a man of great faith because he put his trust in his relationship with God rather than people. He often had to stand alone and speak the prophecies of God. Prophets of God endure much testing by the Holy Spirit so they can withstand the times they must fight the spiritual evil in the land. Your anointing comes and increases as you mature and put your trust and faith in God and what He is doing in you.

---

18. Francis Brown, Samuel Rolles Driver, and Charles Augustus Briggs, Enhanced Brown-Driver-Briggs Hebrew and English Lexicon (Oxford: Clarendon Press, 1977), 458. For the word "glory" from Exodus 33:18.

You grow and change into the image of Christ from glory to glory. That is why obedience is very important. Elijah did not seek God to be a messenger. God chose him. Elijah brought warnings from God and a word of repentance to the kings of the land. His message is just as important today. The prophet Elijah urged the people of Israel to turn from sin to the One true God. A majority of people had already yielded to Satan and his demons through their worship of the Canaanites gods of Baal (sacrifice of babies) and Ashtoreth (fertility goddess). God waited patiently for His people to separate themselves from all the pagan influences and idolatry that surrounded them, as have many today! Today's idols can be riches, fame, lust and pleasures of the flesh, and all perversion that occupies the minds and hearts of humankind. When they refused to obey, God sent Elijah. *Amos 3:7 says, "Surely the Lord God does nothing unless He reveals His secrets to His servants, the prophets."*

Prophets are often hated for the dire messages they bring. They are often accused, as was Elijah, of being the problem. Jezebel and the false prophets of Israel hated Elijah for judging their unrighteousness and spared nothing in their attempts to catch and kill him. Elijah made fierce enemies, but His enemies could not overtake him because he was God's chosen. It may seem in your life that the enemy is trying to overpower you and take you out, but when you know God, and become secure in your identity, Satan's plot to destroy you becomes meaningless! You can't lose! If God is for you, who can be against you *(Psalm 27:1)*?

The wicked King Ahab did more to provoke God to anger than all the other kings who had come before him *(1 Kings 16:33)*. During Ahab's reign, corruption and evil flooded the land. It really sounds like our present times. Ahab and Jezebel would die a humiliating death because of all their wicked deeds against God and their refusal to repent.[19]

The Prophet's Dictionary by Paula A. Price gives a description of the prophetic awaking that I experienced. This is a new prophetic spirit and mantle being awakened by God for service. The awakening involves the Lord's visitation to present Himself as the prophet's covenant God. Usually new prophets, according to *(Numbers 12:6)*, are commissioned through visions and dreams.

The prophetic awakening can be the training and grooming of a chief prophet that leads to an encounter, a spiritual visitation, such as Amos *(Amos 1:1)* and Samuel *(1 Samuel 3:1)*. An awakening is often accompanied by a test assignment or a special object lesson to prepare for the assignment. Sometimes the awakening comes through a human agent, as in the case between Elijah and Elisha. The summons of an older prophet is another way for the prophetic gifting to be awakened by God. Awakening does not immediately make up anointing or appointment. It is simply the first step in a long process whereby the prophet is prepared spiritually, mentally, and practically to serve the Lord at the appointed time. The danger of the prophet's future in the awakening stage is treating the awakening as a release to serve immediately. The training program and its preparatory

19. Life, Hope & Truth. 2022. Chris Moen. [online] Available at: <https://lifehopeandtruth.com/authors/chris-moen/> [Accessed 20 March 2022].

elements are merely stepping stones on the way to installation in the official ministry of a prophet.

In ancient times, the prophets wore mantles that were made out of camel's hair and gathered at the waist with a wide leather belt. Modern day prophet mantles carry the same authority without the need to dress so differently. The mantles of the prophet signify to them the status of authority and station of the officer in the prophetic realm of creation. Both the angelic guard and demonic realm can spiritually see the cloak or mantle of a prophet.

Once your awakening occurs, you become more aware of the natural traits and endowments prophets receive from God to do their jobs. Once this happens, the gifts take on the operational condition. They are now solid tools, weapons of war, rather than soft talents used outside the exercise of the prophet's mantle. More than that, prophetic gifts start out being intermittent and unreliable expressions used casually. Once the training by the Holy Spirit, development, and practice needed for the prophetic competence is complete, the prophet can draw on them to accomplish the purposes assigned to their mantle.

The enemy takes your greatest assets from God and makes them look like your greatest struggle. He perverts your gifts and personality to make you think you are someone you are not. God created me to be a strong and passionate person. I am just a natural born fighter. I was born to fight and overcome the enemy and achieve victory through Christ. As a result of all of my trauma, I would fight with worldly methods (with the flesh and against people). The enemy used hatred, rage, anger, and murder to control me most of my life. I was constantly being tempted to fight the wrong war. If the enemy can deceive you and pervert your thinking about your identity, he knows he can control your reactions and actions through negative circumstances. Soon, you will believe you're always falling short, which is the opposite of what God created you to do. He oppresses you by making you feel like you never measure up, which creates self-hatred. That self-hatred makes you fight against your own identity. The enemy discourages you by keeping you in that same demonic pattern.

We are told to be strong in the Lord and the power of His might *(Ephesians 6:10)*. We cannot lean upon our own understanding *(Proverbs 3:5b)*. Do not put your confidence in your own strength. Your pride will open a door of destruction. Pride and surrender are at odds with each other. We must lay all pride on the altar. You must stay low to soar to higher heights. It is the Lord who has called you to soar higher, so you must set down every encumbering weight because they are from the enemy. Every time you try to take flight, the enemy grabs the strings to pull you back down and frustrate you and keep you stuck.

The eagles of the Lord fly higher than the enemy can operate. The Lord will cut the strings that hold you down. Once and for all, you will soar above the restraints of the enemy. The enemy creates a false plumb-line, which holds many of God's children back. The great I AM will stretch out His strong right arm and cut the cords that have held you back; however, this requires you to humble yourself to His ways, for only He knows the way you're to go on your journey. You must stay close to God. You cannot find the path in your own strength or according to your own plan. The path has been hidden from you. The directions are provided through your total surrender and reliance upon the Holy Spirit. The path to His purpose is narrow, and it's going to become narrower.

The eagle is a prophetic symbol in the Old Testament of Yahweh's prophets. Eagles are extraordinary nurturers that meticulously develop their young. There are two other characteristics one finds in genuine prophets. They are pictured in (*Ezekiel 1:10*) as eternal creatures and (*Job 39:27*) presents them as particularly responsive to the voice of Creator God. The Eagles are also symbolic of a messenger; therefore, it is also applied today to His prophets.[20]

We have been called to the narrow path, but many will not surrender and let the Lord work. They fight and rebel, following their own plans and selfish motivations. Many leave the narrow place thinking it's too hard, not understanding that the path is taking them to glory. As a result, they fall off the path and get lost along the way. That's why we must stay close and stay low because when the surge of His Spirit comes, it will take us to the high place. Stop relying on people to get you to the high place because God alone will exalt you and keep you there in due season. There are few who will allow His spirit to carry them higher.

---

20. Price, P., 2006. The prophet's dictionary. New Kensington, Pa.: Whitaker House, pg. 189, 432

The pressure and resistance causes mantle bearers great duress and fear, which weighs them down and paralyzes them. In your surrender, He will swoop down and cut the cords that entangle you. As the Holy Spirit cuts the cords that bind you, you will help others get free. You will show them spiritual ways and reveal the demonic forces that besiege them. The enemy has tried relentlessly to stop and keep us from entering into our destiny, but he cannot stop us when we are under the shadow and wings of the Almighty and hidden in His secret place. Lay your life down on the altar and you will see more clearly. He will shine a light from Heaven, illuminating the path you should follow. He is the lamp that lights the way that leads you out of the darkness. You have been relying too much on your feelings. Your feelings lead you away from His spiritual truths. His relationship with you is not based on your emotions and your feelings are like sifting sand. His presence is not determined by good works or deeds. It is only by the might and power of the Holy Spirit.

His love is a great work in your heart. You will see it more clearly. His love is what will set you free. His love for you as His child draws you closer in union with Him. Do you trust Him to finish what He has started in you, to bring you into perfection? Remain patient in waiting and watch Him move upon your life. He has chosen you and created you to be different and set you apart. Keep following the leading of His Spirit and He will guide you through the next phase of your journey.

The Lord reveals to you the end of your journey, all while teaching you to overcome all that would hinder you. He constantly tests and lifts your foundation, forming a strong and resilient foundation capable of withstanding any storm the enemy throws at it.

CHAPTER 11

The Giants In Your Land

In *Numbers 13:4-16,* Moses sent one leader from each of the 12 tribes of Israel to serve as "spies." These men were to report on the land and their enemies *(Number 13:17-20).* These men were influential among the people because of their position in Israel. It is always good to take an assessment before assuming new kingdom responsibilities. Ask yourself, "What do I need to know?" Then seek out knowledge and absolute opportunity. Common sense is a valuable aid in accomplishing God's purposes. Moses decided the information that was needed before they entered the promised land. He took careful steps to get the information they needed. God told the Israelites the land was fertile and this land would be theirs.

When the spies reported back to Moses, they gave plenty of good reasons for entering the land, but they could not stop focusing on their fear. They were overwhelmed because they were afraid of their enemies, that they were "like grasshoppers compared to the giants." The enemy does everything he can to make you feel small and insignificant. He will get you to compare your reality instead of the reality in the Word of God. It is so important to stay strong in the Word so when crisis comes, you can combat it with the Word. We must believe in God for the possibility, like Joshua and Caleb. Knowing God is with you is the higher truth that will set you free. Continued focus on the giants, the descendants of Anak, made it easy to forget about God's promise to help. When the chorus of despair went up, everyone joined in. Their greatest fears were being realized. Losing their perspective, the people became caught up in the moment, forgetting what they knew about God. What if the people had spent as much energy moving forward as they did moving backward *(Numbers 13:30-33)*?

They could have enjoyed the land. Their generation never entered it. When a cry of despair goes up, you should consider the larger perspective before you join in. You have better ways to use your energy than to complain. In *(Numbers 11)*, their complaining angered God. How many times do we murmur and complain instead of trusting God and His provision? God performed great miracles while leading the Israelites out of slavery through the desolate desert and up to the very edge of the promised land. He had protected them, fed them, and fulfilled every promise. Yet, when encouraged to take the last step of faith into the land, they refused. After witnessing so many miracles, why did they stop trusting God? Why did they refuse to enter the promised land when they had their goal since leaving Egypt? Simply because they were afraid. Often, we do the same thing. We trust God to handle the smaller issues but doubt His ability to take care of the big problems, the tough decisions, the frightening situations. When facing a tough decision, do not let the negatives cause you to lose sight of the positives. Weigh both sides carefully. Do not let potential difficulties blind you to God's power to help and His promises to guide you. Look to Jesus, the author and finisher of your faith.[21]

The power and promise is in God's Word. We must develop a greater mindset of God, and not allow that tiny God mindset to dictate our future. Caleb saw the same giants and walled city as the other spies, but the ten spies brought back an evil report of unbelief. Caleb's words declared a conviction and a confession before all of Israel: we can overcome. He had surveyed the land, a reminder that faith is not blind. Faith does not deny the reality of difficulty. It declares the power of God in the face of a problem. There is a message in the spirit of Caleb's response to the rejection of his faith filled report. Often we must make decisions that go against popular opinion or demand. Yet, instead of looking at the impossible circumstances, we are called to increase our faith in God's promises. We cannot acquiesce to the sentiment or mood of the times. Spiritual advancement requires faith. Unbelief sees walled cities and giants rather than the presence and the power of God. Unbelief looks at the obstacles. Faith looks to God. Joshua and Caleb did the unpopular thing and called the people to a more positive faith. They led the way

---

21. 1988. Life application Bible. Wheaton, Ill.: Tyndale House.

into the future by confronting a negative report and helping a new generation rise to serve God in faith. Some use their confession of faith to cultivate schism. However, Joshua and Caleb stood their ground in faith and still moved in a partnership and support for 40 years beside many whose unbelief delayed their own experience. What faithful patience! Their eventual actual possession of the land at a later date shows that even though delays come, faith's confession will ultimately bring victory to the believer. The reaction of those who had unbelief was to return to Egypt and kill the two spies that had faith. The ten spies that had the evil report incited rebellion and division among the people.

When such a delay of kingdom benefits occurs, we must stay in a place of consistency doing what the Word of God says! Be persistent in what God is telling you to do. No matter what your circumstances may look like, God will always be faithful. It takes time for Him to bring it all together. It is like putting a puzzle together. Your seeds take time to come forth. When we continually sow faith in our circumstances, we eventually reap that harvest. If you stay continually sowing, you will eventually reap because you reap in this season from what you sowed in the past season. The longer the wait, the larger the blessing! While I am waiting, He is working. While I'm standing, He is preparing the next season.

A giant is any challenge or problem that others may not want to face. They have been hiding from the battle. However, God is stirring you up to take on the giant and defeat the obstacle for a breakthrough. A true champion will take on and defeat the giant before him. You face it straight on and kill it, just like David.

The Philistines used rejection, discouragement, and verbal abuse to stop David. They tried to get him to give up before he even entered the battle with Goliath, but David knew he stood in a place of victory because he knew God. David saw an opportunity when everyone else saw opposition. He did not let fear of man keep him on the sidelines. He had the mindset of a champion because of past victories over his circumstances. The skills he'd perfected had given him the confidence to go into the fight with the giant and see nothing but victory. That is why he won! Don't allow the enemy to cause you to hate where you are in your journey because God will use everything for His good. He knows exactly what it will take to get you to where He is taking you. Do not despise the insignificant times in your walk because every circumstance you overcome is the stepping stone to the next level of your journey. You must learn to enjoy where you are at on the journey.

Goliath used intimidation, mockery, taunting, manipulation, and accusations to create fear and paralyze the army of the Lord. He tried to get them to flee from their assignment of killing the giant. Do not allow the reputation of the enemy or the size of circumstance to keep you from conquering the assignment before you. Nothing is bigger than God. Keep your focus on God, stay surrendered and run the race He has set before you. Keep your focus on the prize you are trying to get. Remember why you have chosen this route and don't turn back from where you are heading.

We must learn to recognize what the giants are in our Promised Land. The power of the Holy Spirit will help you recognize the giants in your land. What are the giants taunting you with? It is usually your greatest struggle or the continuation of a struggle in your family's bloodline. The most important way to overcome the giant is to stop tolerating the giant. Stand strong in kingdom authority. See yourself as winning the victory! Don't tolerate what the enemy is taunting of your family with. Someone must take a stand in your generation.

You have value in the Kingdom, so do not bow down to the enemy. When you take a stand and stop allowing the enemy to intimidate you and shut you down, you will overcome him and receive divine healing. Our confidence must be in God, not man, and not what the enemy is dishing out to us. We cannot look at our circumstances and allow them to be bigger than our God. We cannot allow fear to hold us back any longer. The enemy will push us down and push us out of the race if we do not face the adversity head on.

Whatever the giant in your land, if you don't stand against it and take care of it, it will just get passed down to the next generation. We must partner with the Holy Spirit to confront the giants like David did with Goliath. David had already gained great faith and confidence in the Lord because he had already killed the lion and the bear. He learned God was with him. Through his experiences, he learned God was for him, God was with him, and God was showing him how to defeat the enemy before him. David had learned who God was from every hardship he endured.

His faith grew from every obstacle he overcame while battling from a kingdom mindset, walking in the spirit and not relying on the flesh and not relying on our human strength. The battle belongs to the Lord! We do not fight with carnal weapons, but with spiritual weapons that are capable of pulling down enemy strongholds. We must hold our position and allow God to work. David depended on God. He had a covenant relationship with God. He had learned from previous experiences that the victory belongs to God. He understood the value and the purpose from overcoming each obstacle. He gained knowledge and wisdom through every experience and breakthrough he endured. He did not rely on worldly wisdom or the intellect of man to take him or keep him from doing what God had called him to do. He did not allow people to stifle him, shut him down, or hold him back.

"To the angel of the church in Thyatira write: These are the words of the Son of God, whose eyes are like blazing fire and whose feet are like burnished bronze. I know your deeds, your love and faith, your service and perseverance, and that you are now doing more than you did at first. Nevertheless, I have this against you: You tolerate that woman Jezebel, who calls herself a prophet. By her teaching she misleads my servants into sexual immorality and the eating of food sacrificed to idols. I have given her time to repent of her immorality, but she is unwilling. So I will cast her on a bed of suffering, and I will make those who commit adultery with her suffer intensely, unless they repent of her ways.... To the one who is victorious and does my will to the end, I will give authority over the nations—that one 'will rule them with an iron scepter and will dash them to pieces like pottery'— just as I have received authority from my Father. I will also give that one the morning star (Revelation 2:18-22; 26–28, NIV)."

When your darkest hour lasts a long time. Consider that it may be God developing endurance for your spiritual journey. Trust that God has empowered you for spiritual warfare. God has purified you, baptized you in fire, and shown you how to fight. You have all the resources of Heaven behind you, so arm yourself with the power of God! Long before the enemy targeted you, God chose you for the end-time battle.

CHAPTER 12

The Orphan Spirit

What is an orphan spirit? It's a demonic spirit that invades a person's mind, causing them a sense of abandonment from their past hurts and experiences. It attacks the mind and emotions of the individual suffering with abandonment, rejection, and great disappointment. An orphan spirit attaches to a person who has experienced extreme rejection. It creates separation, worry, anxiety, and fear. Once this spirit enters a person, it becomes a stronghold in their mind and spirit. This controlling spirit will remain until God's Word tears down the stronghold. If this mental fortress is not dismantled, it will continue on to the future generations until it is.

This is a false mindset the enemy puts in place, it does not line up with the truth in God's Word. This orphan spirit is deceitful and makes us feel unaccepted. God's Word tells us that

He will not leave us orphans *(John 14:18)* and we will become as God's children *(2 Corinthians 6:18)*. Take the time to open your heart to the revelation of God's love for you. Change the direction of your bloodline back to fellowship with God. Allow Him to heal and cleanse your heart. This could be your missing link to freedom.

I experienced so much emotional turmoil from the enemy's false religious thinking. Wanting freedom for myself and my family kept me searching for the truth. An orphan spirit is an identity that separates us from the perfect love of Jesus. Jesus paid a high price for our redemption; we are kidnapped royalty. Upon salvation, we begin a personal relationship with Christ. Our ransom is paid. God's love and acceptance of us stood before we were formed in our mother's womb. God created us to belong and to be treasured. Only the Father's presence can heal the orphan spirit.

So much of the body of Christ is feeling a lack of love and true acceptance by God. This is a physical sign in the natural of what needs to happen spiritually. The spirit of adoption is the manifestation of the spirit of God and a prophetic declaration of healing and restoration back to sonship. The sons and daughters of God are being awakened in this hour to their rightful place in the Kingdom of God. We will come into our full inheritance as God's children when our restoration is completed.

The orphan spirit makes you see others through the lens of deeply rooted resentment and anger because, subconsciously, you are angry with your absent father. This taints your perception of other male figures in your life, including God, the Father. Once abandoned or rejected by your earthly father, a deep void is created. Broken trust with your earthly father then makes it difficult for us to interact with your heavenly Father. We need that breach to be healed to bring restoration back to us as His children. Knowing the father's love is especially necessary for a believer to function as a healthy member of society and as a member of the body of Christ.

I have some questions for you to consider. The answer to these questions will give you a better understanding of the grip the orphan spirit has over you.

- Do I make choices out of insecurities?
- Am I jealous of other people's success?
- Do I try to earn God's love with works?
- Do I self-protect by drawing inward?
- Do I feel unworthy or not good enough?
- Do I try to fulfill it with work, physical appearance, self-gratification, narcissistic behavior, or self- indulgent behavior?
- Am I driven to success and have the mindset I will succeed at all costs?
- Do I use people to fulfill my goals?
- Do I repel my children or my spiritual children?
- Do I struggle with anger and fits of rage?
- Do other people in my family struggle with anger and rage? This could be a generational curse.
- Do I always compete with others?
- Do I lack self-esteem?

- Do I see my identity in possessions, physical appearance, activities, or work?
- Do I strive for perfection?
- Do I primarily identify myself through my career, title, material possessions, sports activities, or pleasures?
- Do I place the value of my identity in these lies and deceptions of the enemy?

I know I did for most of my life. As you become aware and recognize the attributes and limits the enemy has placed on you, I pray that you refuse to allow this spirit access to your mind by taking every ungodly thought captive.

Here are some attributes of how this spirit operates. It affects all aspects of your decisions and relationships. I struggled with so many of these symptoms. God has taken me through a process of awareness in order to bring healing and freedom.

- Addiction
- Self-indulgent behaviors through overeating, sex, lust, shopping, etc.
- Always searching for the meaning in life and searching for contentment.
- Jealousy, envy, disobedience, rebellion, abandonment, loneliness, isolation, alienation, drawing inward, rejection.
- A critical spirit of other and self, very defensive about everything.
- Always blaming others for what is wrong.

- You are unable to receive correction from anyone and are not teachable.
- You operate out of the fear of always feeling unworthy and not good enough.
- You feel unloved with constant thoughts of self-hatred because of failures and sins.

Many are unaware they are functioning emotionally with an orphan spirit. Even though you are adopted as God's sons and daughters, you are unaware of what this spirit is doing to you, and how it is controlling you.

An orphan spirit will limit your capacity to understand your identity and purpose. You won't be able to maximize all that God has for you in your Kingdom purpose.

God's love brings security, rest, and citizenship. Love is who God is; not only how He acts, but His consistency covers our inconsistency. He declares us lovable.

We are His image and that image is love. To love and to be loved. Only the Spirit of God can bring us revelation of the Father's heart towards us. Only the Father can make us whole again and set us free from the orphan spirit.

Revelation is the first step in overcoming this spirit. We have to deny this spirit access to our lives. Recognize the patterns and cycles the enemy uses against you. They are usually the same rejection and abandonment situations. You must see what the enemy has done to you. If you refuse to admit the existence of the spirit and its operation in your life, it will be impossible for you to get free. You must bring all your past hurts and feelings of abandonment to God and ask for healing. Ask Jesus to stand with you in your past hurts and reach out to Him for full restoration. Join me in this prayer and allow God to work on your behalf to set you free! Your freedom is His desire. Surrender all to God. Allow Jesus access to your wounded heart, to all the dead places in your heart. He will make you whole and set you free. That is my hope for all who read this.

PRAYER:

Father God, help me realize I am struggling to connect with you because of the rejection and abandonment that I have experienced in my past. I ask you to start the healing process that I so desperately need. Clean out the things in my life that are holding me back from a deeper relationship with you. Help me recognize the open doors to this spirit, help me see and identify those things that are hindering my identity and purpose in you. Father, forgive me for not being able to feel and receive your love, the unconditional love that you have for me. I ask you to forgive me for assuming that you are the same as the others that have hurt me. Please help me overcome the orphan spirit!

Jesus, please forgive me for embracing the attitudes and the actions of an orphan spirit. I want to experience your love and heart's desire for me. I am a part of a healthy spiritual family. I break all soul ties that I have formed with an orphan spirit. I bind my body, heart and spirit to God's will and purpose for my life, in Jesus' name. Lord, I ask that you heal me from the spirits of abandonment and rejection. I break all soul ties with all that has formed in my mind and emotions from an orphan spirit. I put the blood of Jesus on the origin of where an orphan spirit came into my life. I recognize and renounce the orphan spirit that has gained access and control over my life and bloodline. I break its power and control by the power of the blood of Jesus. I break the generational curse now. I repent for my ancestors on my mother's and father's side who took part with this spirit. I put the blood of Jesus on the root where it came in. With heavenly power, burn away every root and branch connected to it. I declare it broken and to no affect to me or any future generations from this day forward.

God, please help me have the heart and mindset of a son and daughter. As your child, help me turn my heart toward you, Heavenly Father, and heal my relationship with my earthly father. Send me a spiritual father handpicked by you. Lord, help me pray for and support all spiritual fathers that you have placed in my life. Please help me model the attitude and heart that Jesus showed towards you. Please reveal to me all the wounded areas of my heart. Heal those areas and make me whole. Lord, I ask that you help me forgive every spiritual father who wounded or failed me. Lord, please help me commit to a church and a spiritual father. In Jesus' name Amen.

SCRIPTURE REFERENCES:

Concerning the Orphan Spirit:

Romans 8:14-15

Galatians 4:4-7

Philippians 4:6

1 Timothy 2:14

Romans 5: 12-19

Jeremiah 31:3

Psalm 68:5-6

Psalm 146:9

John 14:18

Ephesians 1:5-6

CHAPTER 13

Spirit of Offense

"Then He said to the disciples, *"It is impossible that no offenses should come, but woe to him through whom they do come! It would be better for him if a millstone were hung around his neck, and he were thrown into the sea, than that he should offend one of these little ones (Luke 17:1–2, NKJV)."*

"I have life experiences fighting the spirit of offense. When you become offended, you begin to see yourself as a victim. No one can deny that words hurt, but are you going to remain in that moment and allow your spiritual enemy to torment you? Or will you join with the Holy Spirit and allow Him to protect and strengthen you? We can ask for God's perspective. When feelings are raging, recognize that it is just temptation from the enemy. We can choose to stop the enemy in his tracks and not let him gain access to us by practicing separation and reflecting on God's truth.

Consider this vision from my friend Robin. She saw a waiter with a tray of very appetizing desserts. He was going to each person, trying to get them to buy a dessert. Each serving seemed to reflect the wounds in your soul. Which one do you prefer? Shall it be this or that? That is what the enemy does. He makes offense look like it's just and right and we deserve to be upset.

What excites the spirit of offense in your spirit?
- Do you find yourself ensnared and entangled by a web of emotions?
- Do you get your feelings hurt (offended) easily?
- Do you jump to conclusions?
- Are your thoughts and stories dwelling on past hurts, past circumstances, betrayals?
- Are you always rehearsing your traumas?
- Do you suffer from the same issues over and over?
- Do you have guilt because you can't overcome something?
- Are you caught up in repetitive cycles?

Many individuals don't suffer trauma at the hands of strangers, but from family members. It is a fact of life that someone will hurt us, but we're never expected to live with constant fear and guilt. God expects us to be overcomers, not lifelong victims. When we see ourselves as victims, we lose sight of our identity and God's perspective about who He says we are in Christ.

When you draw proper and healthy boundaries through discernment, love, and forgiveness, you give God something to work with towards healing and deliverance. Offense requires forgiveness of self and others. If you have allowed offense to take root, you must repent. When you choose to be offended and unforgiving, you are coming into agreement with the enemy and helping him do his job better. Rehearsing every bad situation that has happened to you in your life over and over gives him access to attack your life through the open wounds in your soul.

You are wide open for attacks from legion because you are dwelling among the tombs. Legion is a group of demons. *Mark 5:9 says, "And Jesus asked him, "What is your name?" He said, "Legion, for we are many."* This scripture is about the exorcism of the Gerasene demoniac. It's an account in the New Testament of an incident in which Jesus performs an exorcism (*Matthew 8:28-34 ESV, Luke 8:26-39 ESV*).

Be transparently honest before God and he can heal your heart. You are a child of God. You are an overcomer. When you recall and replay situations of deep hurt and pain, you open yourself up for torment and self-pity. Use those memories to pray for that person and talk to God about it. Let's evaluate what we think and say about ourselves. This will show the brokenness in our hearts and our spirits.

"The eyes of the LORD are everywhere, keeping watch on the wicked and the good — (Proverbs 15:3, NIV)."

"A cheerful heart is good medicine, but a crushed spirit dries up the bones —(Proverbs 17:22, NIV)."

Cycles of offense keep us broken-hearted and crushed in spirit. When caught in the same cycle of emotional pain, we keeps ourselves connected to the past. Offense is our response to the open wounds and broken spirit. Our actions, choices and words reflect what's on the inside of us, even though others can't see it. Outwardly, it is a direct reflection of the wounds that live in our hearts. The Lord cannot heal us and set us free because we are allowing the enemy in through the same cycles of offense. We continue to be broken in spirit and operate out of the wrong heart motive, which allows other spirits to operate against us. The spirit of the PAST keeps us from the future. We then continue in a cycle of regret, wishing that we would or wouldn't have, or should or shouldn't have, which depletes our spirit. We then look inward and think of everything we are not; it hinders our true identity.

The Word of God is the sword of the spirit; a sword we use in war. The Lord will teach you to yield the sword. You will use it to defeat the enemies of your soul. You will learn to use it correctly and see glorious victories. His Word is the source of our understanding the warfare in which we are involved. We gain wisdom and strategy in the Word. The Lord will show us great and mighty things in His Word to overcome the battle before us. "Faith in the heart that is released through the mouth can move mountains (John Eckhardt)."

PRAYER

Father, in the name of the Lord Jesus Christ, by the authority given to me to bind and loose, I bind every evil spirit that has come in because of experiences of the past. I cast off all hurt, bitterness, guilt, and blocked emotions. The effects of bad memories keep me from receiving your love and acceptance. I command these spirits to come out, and I decree freedom for my emotions in the name of the Lord Jesus Christ.

CHAPTER 14

Unforgiveness

Unforgiveness is an alignment issue of the heart. It will take you out of alignment, blocking your spirit from hearing God. How often do you get offended? Do you get your feelings hurt easily? Do you jump to conclusions? Are your thoughts or stories always dwelling on the past? Do you dwell on those who have hurt, betrayed, or abused you? This pain is a direct reflection of the wounds in your soul and the unforgiveness that dwells there.

Fear, resentment, stewing, hostility, anger, rage, bitterness, malice, evil speaking, wanting revenge or holding a grudge are all great indications that you are operating in unforgiveness. These spirits work together to keep you in bondage. When we do not cleanse and release these hurts and wounds from our soul, it creates strongholds in our minds. A stronghold chang- es our perception, and we believe the lies of the accuser. The enemy uses deception to get us to believe that things are worse than what they are, or that things happened in a way other than the way it actually did happen. The enemy twists and taints our perception. I'm not trying to downplay anything you have gone through. Bitterness and strife are productive giants to unforgiveness!

Here are some ways to tell if unforgiveness is stuck in our hearts! Taken from (*Luke 15:29*) and Author RT Kendall:

1. Always keeps score?
2. Always boast of his own record?
3. Always complains?
4. I did all the work, usually a workaholic?
5. Legalism, divides, separates, and alienates himself from others?
6. Accuses, exposes, and continues to bring up the offense?
7. Always angry and jealous whenever someone else gets blessed?
8. See's everyone's offense except their own?

If we are all honest, we can find ourselves somewhere on this list.

"Exercise foresight and be on the watch to look [after one another], to see that no one falls back from and fails to secure God's grace [his unmerited favor and spiritual blessing], in order that no root of resentment [rancor, bitterness, or hatred] shoots forth and causes trouble, and many become contaminated and defiled by it." — *(Hebrews 12:15 Amplified Bible)*

The enemy will use the people in our lives to catch us off guard and offend us. The enemy will keep us in a repetitive cycle of bondage to throw us off the course God has designed for us. It robs us of our strength, joy, peace, and health. There are studies that show how unforgiveness directly affects sickness and cancer in your body. The next testimony will provide an example of the connection between unforgiveness and disease in the physical body.

DORIS' TESTIMONY

A Christian lady named Doris came into our shop to get her hair done by Carlen, a stylist in my salon. She told her she was having some heart issues and needed prayer. Carlen and several other people gathered to pray for her health. I was praying in my spiritual prayer language and I received a word of knowledge that Doris had unforgiveness. I asked her and she answered really quickly, "No." I then asked, "Are you sure?" She answered, "Yes."

We kept praying, each person taking a turn. The Holy Spirit wouldn't let me move on about the unforgiveness, so I asked her again! "Doris, are you sure you don't have unforgiveness?" Once again, she answered, "No." I quietly said, "God, I know I heard you right." He said, "Yes." So I immediately said, "Doris, the Lord said that you do have unforgiveness." She looked up at me with surprised eyes, nodded, and finally admitted that she did. She said, "It is my sister." We explained about the power and the release from forgiving and she said, "I am going to have to think and pray about this."

When she came in the following month, she asked us to gather around her. She had something to tell us. She decided to forgive her sister and called her. They had a joyous reunion, but most importantly, all of her heart tests came back normal. She was praising God. About a year after their reunion, Doris's sister got sick and died quickly and unexpectedly. Doris said that she was so thankful to have that year with her sister before she died. She also stated that she would have never forgiven herself had she not forgiven herself for not forgiving her sister.

What if your offense/pain is continually reoccurring or lasting years and the Lord tells you that you can't leave? Physical, emotional, verbal, and sexual abuse, and adultery are not okay. These situations need to have immediate attention, intervention, and possible separation.

You've prayed, fasted, cried, stood, given up, and prayed some more for many years with minimal results. What if when you cried out to God to deal with the person mistreating you and His response was always, "We aren't going to be talking about them right now! We are going to talk about you, your behavior, and your response to the situation." I really had a hard time adjusting to that statement. I thought it was unfair because I could clearly see they had the problem, not me.

What if God spoke and said the person you are dealing with is operating out of their own brokenness? What if you considered the foul spirits in operation instead of the person themselves? Would this change your perspective? For the first time, it changed mine. I saw the person God created instead of the mean person who wasn't being nice to me. It wasn't easy, but in tears I again cried out to the Lord, and again He answered.

I had to detach myself emotionally and pray for him just like I did for any other person. This seemed to help because I had a hard time praying. I was always angry for the mistreatment I was subjected to received. Things started improving and changing for him and for me. Over time, things became pretty decent. However, it was still very frustrating because he refused to agree with anything. He was continually working against me for everything I suggested, spiritually or personally. Last September at our annual Cleansing Stream healing and deliverance meetings at my church, I was fasting and praying about this block that I had been struggling with in my prophetic gift. There was a dam of some sort keeping it from flowing smoothly. This had been going on for five years. Something was out of alignment. I did not recognize it, but my flesh was over my spirit.

One night I had three dreams in a row. The first was a little alarming. I was watching myself kneeling by a tub in the bathroom. I was getting ready to wash my hair. I reached to turn the water on and heard a voice warn me to be watchful of something or someone. I told the voice, "Oh, I am aware of it." I washed my hair under the water. As I sat up, I sensed something evil had entered the room. One grabbed my right arm. One grabbed my left arm and the other one grabbed my legs and feet. I struggled with them, but I was powerless and couldn't move. I woke up very disturbed and shook up. All I could think was, "Wow, what was that all about!" I prayed and went back to sleep and had another dream. That was the first time that I fell back to sleep and had a sequence of dreams.

In the second dream, my husband and I lived in a mobile home in a trailer park. I was returning home to find people taking the trailer apart to be moved. I was upset because I was unaware that anything was going on. I went inside to find out what happened, and we were being evicted. I was so mad because my husband said he just hadn't been paying the pad rent. I was trying to figure out something to do, so I asked the people to stop disassembling the trailer until I could figure out a solution but they would not. I called my dad and asked for help but knew he wouldn't help.

When he told me that he wouldn't help, I cried, and I felt so overwhelmed with disappointment. I then screamed at my husband. How could you do this? How could you let this happen? How could you just not make the payments? I choked him around his neck, full of rage. The landlord was there also, and I choked her as well. My behavior shocked and scared me because I couldn't control it! I then asked for an extension and she agreed to one month until August. We owed $2000. My daughter-in-law gave me the checkbook.

Unfortunately, I didn't write down the 3rd dream, but I knew immediately what the first dream meant. The bathroom was the equivalent of cleansing or purification. Washing hair symbolized the cleansing or changing of negative thoughts and bad ideas. It was the process of getting a fresh start to rid myself of unpleasant thoughts. The demonic forces at work were rage and bitterness.

The second dream represented the broken dreams and promises of an absentee father: the abandonment, and lack of support. The mobile home didn't rest on a fixed foundation. It was a temporary residence indicating low self-esteem. The experience of being evicted exemplified the feelings of helplessness, neglect, irresponsible behavior, and complacency. The new beginning starts with faith and paying the back rent. The time was now at hand for a new realized victory over my circumstances that the enemy stacked up against me.

The lesson I received from these dreams stemmed from the access I was giving to rage and bitterness in my life. The doorway I left open for this orphan spirit was frustration with my dad and husband. I never really got rid of those spirits! It became one of those repetitive cycles holding me in bondage. I was working on autopilot, just coasting along, dealing with whatever bump came along. I was merely surviving because it was all I knew how to do. Through these dreams, God revealed deeply hidden painful areas of my heart with the promise of change to come.

BITTERNESS

We must refuse to let bitterness take root in our hearts or allow ourselves to be offended or remain angry (Ephesians 4:26-27). This means we cannot follow our feelings; we must press past our feelings in order to do what God asks of us. Our spirit and not our flesh must lead us. If we are struggling in this area, God's grace will disintegrate the deep roots that entangle us. We must admit we have others to forgive and choose to forgive! We have a choice: bow to our feelings or to the Word of God. We have to be quick to choose forgiveness.

If you do not forgive, then you are deciding to live with the enemy instead of defeating the giant before you! Many times, forgiveness is a test of the heart. We must pass this test before the Lord. Forgiveness opens our hearts to the love of the Father and everyone around us! While praying for people, I often felt many had layers of hurts and wounds that God wanted to come to terms with! Trust Him again! He loves you and wants you healed, free, and walking in victory!

What is forgiveness? The Encyclopedia of the Bible defines it as,

- to pardon
- to lift up
- bear
- to take away
- forgive
- to cover
- to let pass
- to wash
- to purify[22]

---

22. https://www.biblegateway.com/resources/encyclopedia-of-the-bible/Forgiveness

Rudolf Bultmann in The Theological Dictionary of the New Testament describes it in this manner.

- "The word "forgiveness" used in *Matthew 26:28 (NASB)* is ἀφιέναι,
- "to send off," is from an early period, and used in every nuance, both literally. and figuratively.,
- from "to hurl" (e.g., missiles) to "to release,"
- "to let go,"
- or "to let be."[23]
- It may have either a material or a personal object...
- To be emphasized is the legal use much attested in
- "to release someone from a legal relation," whether office, marriage, obligation, or debt...."

We need to forgive because God said so! (*Matthew 18:33-35*) it's in your notebook. If you don't forgive, God won't forgive you (*Matthew 6:15*)! Your faith won't work. Your prayers, which are [our fellowship with the father] your healing and blessing will be blocked! God's Word says He will turn us over to the tormentors [demons] when we flat out refuse to obey and forgive.

"Then said he unto the disciples, It is impossible but that offenses will come: but woe unto him, through whom they come!" (*Luke 17:1, AV*)

FOUR DIRECTIONS FOR FORGIVENESS:
1. God's forgiveness of us
2. Our forgiveness of others
3. Our forgiveness of ourselves

23. Bultmann, Rudolf, and Robert Morgan. Theology of the New Testament. Waco, TX: Baylor University Press, 2007.

4.   Our forgiveness of God

FORGIVENESS IS A PROCESS:
1.   Coming into alignment is a process
2.   Walking in alignment is a process
3.   True forgiveness is a process
4.   We must break unhealthy soul ties, which are the joining together of two people with the same purpose or heart.
5.   Consider any vows made…"I'm not going to be like them," or "I'll never (fill in the blank)," etc.
6.   Consider anyone you may have hurt or offended

HOW DO WE FORGIVE?
1.   Acknowledge the hurt or offense. Big or little, we must deal with it.
2.   Respond to a decision from your heart to obey God.
3.   Consecrate the person and the hurt to the Lord, and ask Him for His mercy-grace.
4.   If you have allowed the offense to take root, you must repent.
5.   Pray and bless them from your heart, even if you don't feel it.

When someone offends or hurts you, pray for them immediately. Don't curse them with your words, which is witchcraft. STOP talking about the person and the offense. Stop dwelling on it and pray!

FORGIVING OURSELVES

In using my own life, for example, I really felt the need to go into greater detail in this section. When we pray for people, this is one of the common areas where people struggle the most. The enemy starts attacking us in the womb or at a very young age. He begins between the ages of three to five years old. It is so important to keep your children and grandchildren covered with the blood of Jesus in prayer.

The reason why the enemy is able to target your children at such a young age is spiritual neglect. In every aspect of our family's lives, we must be proactive, and spiritual protection should be at the top of the list. There are ways in which we can begin to provide spiritual protection and teach children that are so important.

First, provide a consistent, Christian, biblically based spiritual covering. Search for and begin attending church regularly as a family. When your family does not attend church or has never attended church, this leaves you a wide-open target for the enemy to attack. The best defense against a spiritual attack is a spiritually proactive offense.

Second, the habits of the grandparents and parents follow to the grandchildren and children. We all pick up the looks, quirks, and habits of our family members. Some of those "quirks" are harmless and might be a little silly. But a spiritual, generational curse has eternal consequences and can lead to destruction. Some of these generational curses can be learned or accepted behavior. Some examples could be all types of abuse, anger, abandonment, addictions, fear, stress worry, addiction, suicide, anger, strife, murder, perversion [molestation, masturbation, pornography], lust, adultery, and poverty. Take an inventory of these behaviors and seek the spiritual empowerment to break them.

When you choose to sin and come into agreement with the enemy, you are giving him access to attack your life. Do not blame your grandparents. Take responsibility for your own spiritual wellness by confessing and then repenting of your sin. This will begin healing your soul and close the doors to attacks from the enemy. I'm telling you this to show you how these things affect you and your family's personal lives and decisions.

TACTICS THE ENEMY USES AGAINST YOU

The enemy will use a cycle of circumstances to create a dependent vulnerability that leaves us wounded, broken, and open to attack. These attacks leave us filled with regret, guilt, condemnation, and unworthiness. We are ashamed of what we have done or what has happened to us. When enemy assaults add to the condemnation, we believe it because we are already feeling bad about our actions. Coming into agreement with the enemy only makes it easier for him to do his job. It paralyzes us and keeps us from moving forward. Don't stay stuck in the past; ashamed of what has happened or what you have done. The enemy assaults us in our minds over and over. We must realize these are false accusations, guilt, and shame because God didn't put them there.

Don't add your guilt to Jesus' sacrifice. Believe what He did for you on the cross! He died for you to be forgiven and free. Make a choice to receive your gift for yourself! A gift of forgiveness! It's still your choice! Repent for agreeing with the enemy. If there is someone you have wronged, repent, and ask the Holy Spirit to lead you in handling that situation. Sometimes we have to apologize to make it right and other times, He will have us handle it differently.

FORGIVING GOD

Are there obvious areas that you can see where you are mad at God? Trying to understand the pain can often lead us to harden our hearts towards God. When things are not making sense, we view God through our own perception, which is through man's image and not God's heavenly image. God is not a man, so not understanding the Word of God or His ways leaves us open to deceptive mental attacks by the enemy. God's ways are not our ways! There were so many things I didn't understand about God or the journey. The Lord often spoke to me. My very strong gift of discernment and a prophetic gift became my lifeline to the Father. I learned very early to listen to the Holy Spirit. I have always tried to be led by the Spirit of God and not my flesh.

To be honest, I am surprised at the anger I feel rising in my heart as I reflect on my life and all that I have been through. I have often wondered how God could have allowed what has happened to me for so many years. As tears flowed down my cheeks, I realized I need this as much as anyone.

CHURCH HURT

The war had been waging on with no end in sight. I had become weary, and lost sight of where I was going. The enemy threw assault after assault year after year without end. My prayers went unanswered. My circumstances were unchanged. The only one who seemed to be advancing was the enemy. I just didn't understand, and I resented everything going on. I have to admit I'm just now realizing that I have resented God because of what I endured. I experienced one betrayal after another. One person after another told lies about me; accusation after accusation. It was painful and almost more than I could take. I had little or no guidance along the way, except for the leading of the Holy Spirit which has proved to be so merciful and gracious. I am truly amazed at all the Father has brought me through, leading and guiding me through songs, dreams, and His Word. In the past few years, He has graciously placed people in my path to help and guide me, to pray with and for me, and to encourage me along my journey to freedom. I must admit sometimes pushing and pulling because I was a tad bit resistant.

The hardest thing I had to endure was being hurt by church leadership. When I found a loving church family, I truly thought it would be a safe place and the last place I would encounter brokenness and betrayal. Please understand the enemy is like a roaring lion seeking whomever he can devour and unfortunately, the church isn't exempt (*1 Peter 5:8*). The following is the story of that betrayal and how God brought me through it.

I had a dream that a clown was hugging my sister. It looked at me and said, "YOU BETTER SHUT YOUR MOUTH." I woke up with the Holy Spirit all over me like a shield of protection. I knew it was the enemy, but I did not know what was coming. I had a friend for about 17 years. Our families were very close. I felt as if the Lord wanted me to distance myself from her because of some strife and personal problems she was having. It was just a draining situation. I pulled back, and of course, she didn't take it well. We worked at the same shop together, so it was difficult. She did several of the leaders' hair from church and some of the congregation. I knew she had been talking because they had started treating me differently. It ended up where we weren't talking much at all. I remained cordial, but it was rocky.

She was about nine months pregnant, and the Lord started waking me up with a burden to pray for her and her baby every night. This went on for two weeks. In the process, five people came up and ask about her and her baby. I heard they were okay. They also had a burden to pray as well. Three of us got together and prayed for her. One lady had a vision of this demon trying to push her into this fiery pit. We were a little freaked out. This was more than what we were used to dealing with. I called the church pastor to get some advice. There was only one in the office that day. The pastor was one of her clients. I told him everything that was going on. He told me he would pray about it and get back to me. After two weeks, I assumed he hadn't taken it seriously. I called her husband, sharing the burden with him, imploring him to pray for his wife and baby! He said he had been feeling the same way. That night, the burden left.

I guess about a week after that, the pastor asked me to meet him at church and to bring my husband. I thought this cannot be a good thing, but we went. Boy was I right! As we sat across the desk from him, he told me that what I was doing was not from God. He accused me of conjuring up evil spirits and putting curses on this woman and her baby. He expressed that God didn't give warnings like that. He said he spoke with her and her husband and told them such. I was shocked. I had poured my heart out for three weeks in prayer for her. I cried in disbelief. Could this really be happening? My poor husband didn't know what to say. He was brought up Catholic, so I think part of him was questioning if there was some truth here. He didn't understand.

Remember the anger I mentioned earlier? Well I was considering jumping across the desk and punching him. To be honest, I knew he was only doing this because she cut his hair and he was trying to defend her. My husband then came over and touched my shoulder and told him there must be some misunderstanding. He said that I loved God with all my heart and that's all I was seeking. He knew I had been praying for this lady with concern. We left; it was so bad for me. I told God I did nothing wrong. I was expecting an apology from the pastor. I just stood on that.

My husband and I went and met with the senior pastors and explained the situation to them. God bless my husband. He did most of the talking. I told them the vision wasn't even mine. Someone else had it. I had explained the dream I had first. They explained the enemy was trying to shut me up. The other, much younger pastor did not have the same gifts and didn't understand my gifts. I did get an apology from the first pastor we met with. He was very humble and sorry. I was very thankful to the Lord. Oh, and I went to the theater with my grandson to see Jonah the next day and guess what? God was sending Jonah to Nineveh to warn them of impending danger! God is so good!

During this time, God would not release me to go to another church. I went every Sunday but was feeling worse each week. My husband stopped going after that. When I complained to God, He said, "Are you going there for the people or for me?" I said, "You." God answered, "Then go and just worship me, no matter how anyone else treats you!" Whew, that was hard! There were only a few who were nice, but I wanted to be in God's will, so I obeyed.

I thought things were looking up, right? Wrong! During my prayer time, the Lord revealed something personal about another pastor, so I just sent them an email and tried to explain what I saw and what I thought it meant. It wasn't bad, just deep. After that I was isolated even more. I was refused admission to prayer teams, women's teams, and door greeter. No one said anything to me. I really didn't understand what I'd done wrong. I asked God to tell me what was going on.

Several years had passed until one day my group leader asked me to go to lunch. She told me I had a reputation for being a false prophet. She did not agree and wanted to repair the relationship between me and the church leaders. I was floored! I just couldn't believe it! Is this really happening...again?

This leader was coming with the purest of hearts and all sincerity, but it didn't hurt any less. I cried and cried and cried! I trusted these people so much, I thought surely if I was doing something wrong, they would at least tell me to my face. So, I set up a meeting with one of the senior pastors and spoke with him. He said he was unaware of anything going on and he would get back to me but never did. The person trying to help me was subjected to some backlash. I was searching for answers and the truth. I was crushed! How could the pastors that had prophesied over my life for so many years be saying this now? I got the prophecies out and read them, asking God, "So what is the truth?" I was confused!

God had told me I could not go to another church, so I decided not to go to church at all for about a year and a half. That was also very difficult. I don't recommend this! I was miserable. God is blameless. He never changes. We blame Him instead of the enemy, our choices, sins, etc.

A women's pastor I was close to got wind of the situation and made all efforts to understand the situation. I was thankful for her and her loving heart in the matter. I went to church again. God worked in me! Wouldn't you know, I saw the person who hurt me at church the same month. I knew it was a forgiveness test! She had not been to church for 8-9 years.

When we get overwhelmed from the battles in which we are engaged, we have allowed our spiritual self to disconnect from our life source. That is when a person becomes spiritually indifferent, hopeless, and despairing in life. It is the Spirit of God that sustains and upholds us.

Pain affects our perspective on how we view others and how others view us! When we filter everything through our past hurts, rejections, and experiences, we find it impossible to believe what God's Word says about us. It directly affects your relationship with the Father, how you view and receive His Word, His faithfulness, goodness, and love. If you cannot receive His love, then you have no love to give away to those around you. The knowledge of God's Word without love is a destructive force because it puffs us up with pride and legalism. This causes us to justify ourselves rather than repent of unforgiveness. In forgiveness, you are showing your love for God and your love for man. May you learn to love freely again.

Through discouragement, become an encourager. Through your weakness become a warrior! About a year ago, I heard the Lord say, "Come to my altar. Come past the outer courts! Come back to me!" I knew God was looking for a greater intimacy with me, but I just couldn't press in. I thought it was because of the backlash I received from the enemy before, but now I realize that deep within my heart I had been angry at the Lord. I realize He is saying, "You can go to church and not really live in the presence of God!" The veil separated us from God, but Jesus died and tore the veil so we could enter the most Holy Place with the Father. It's your choice to stay in the outer courts with anger, bitterness, and unforgiveness! When you are mad all the time, you cannot move past the outer courts and into the Father's house. You must decide today to forgive in order to enjoy life and live in His promise.

We live in perilous times and the Bible says, *"And then many will be offended and repelled and will begin to distrust and desert [him whom they ought to trust and obey] and will stumble and fall away and betray one another and pursue one another with hatred. And many false prophets will rise up and lead many into error. And the love of the great body of people will grow cold because of the multiplied lawlessness and iniquity (Matthew 24:10-12 Amp)."*

People of God, the great body is the church, not the world. Refuse to let your love grow cold! Stir up the love in your life towards your spouse, family, friends, neighbors, coworkers and the unlovable. God has put us on earth for a reason. The difficulty of love is exactly what enables it to be so powerful! When we have no choice about who we love, love becomes harder. The Bible tells in *1 Peter 1:22, "...love one another deeply."* This is a very deliberate action. This is the love of the Father and the love He calls us to have one for another.

CHAPTER 15

Patterns and Cycles of Jezebel

As I submitted to the Holy Spirit, my life changed through a series of dreams. He showed me repeated cycles of sin, behavior, emotions, and attacks that were all connected through a demonic structure created to destroy me. I was fighting the same battles for years, caught in the same vicious cycles, but I couldn't recognize what the enemy was doing. I will share with you how the cycles of Jezebel attacked continually until I fought back God's way.

The battle ultimately belongs to the Lord. He will fight for you, but you still have a part to play. He cannot do your part for you. Only you can! Don't enlist others to fight for you because it will only set you back. Engage your will with His and He will teach you how to overcome the attacks. When you find yourself in a battle with chaos raging all around you, He wants you to use your authority in Christ to defeat the enemy. Don't continue to stay stuck trying to figure it out. In your natural mind, it's a complete waste of time because it's a spiritual war. I allowed myself to become a prisoner of war because I went AWOL. Then I started to see myself as Christ sees me. Whatever you overcome, you have a resident anointing to help others overcome, which is exactly why I've written this book.

Right out of the gate, this demonic spirit muzzled me with fear and intimidation. It is such a bully and knew exactly where to hit me and what my weaknesses were. When you carry a prophetic anointing, a Jezebel spirit will target you. It all started with a dream.

MIND CONTROL

The enemy of your soul sets out to steal, kill, and destroy you *(John 10:10)*! Make no mistake. The enemy hates you, everything about you because of who made you. The enemy is jealous of your position with the Father in Heaven. He assaults you in every way possible by creating chaos with battles in your mind. He fights unfairly to win the war over your mind. The spirit of mind control wants to occupy, hinder, and arrest the development of every believer and block the unbeliever from truly seeing and accepting Christ.

We must learn and understand how these spirits operate to gain control and take up occupancy in our mind, will, and emotions. The enemy was attacking me from every direction and in every area in my life: marriage, family, relationships, friends, finances, and church hurt. The struggles were overwhelming and kept me in a whirlwind of fog because I didn't have a clue what was happening or why.

In my early 20s, I found myself in a stress center for eight weeks, not knowing how to deal with life or how to move on. It was my darkest hour. I thought I had found a better way of life than I had known, only to be brokenhearted again. The enemy hit me out of nowhere by destroying the family that I was trying to build. I had so much stress and worry about the future. I was afraid and felt like I had nobody to turn to.

For the first time in my life, I knew fully that I was lost and barely holding on. I was used to being in control, the one everyone counted on, who helped hold it all together. I wanted to hold it together for my small children because I didn't want them to grow up in the turmoil I did. I was so tired of fighting and trying to control people, situations, and circumstances so I could keep them all from falling apart. I had to admit that I was having a mental breakdown and needed some help. The stress center was a stepping-stone to the journey in rebuilding my relationship with the Lord. Going there was part of the healing process I needed because I learned other people are not responsible for your happiness. True happiness only comes from the Lord.

I had to take off the mask that I was hiding behind and admit where I was and what my struggles were. I had to swallowing my pride and admit what I was trying so desperately to hide.

We must face and accept what is going on in our lives. Face your demons head on instead of stroking them. You may not think that other people see your struggles, but in reality, people can see more than you realize and your Father in Heaven sees everything.

The enemy kept bombarding my mind with relentless racing thoughts. The thoughts told me I was a horrible person. The enemy's enlisted friends, enemies, and even family members to tell me that, as well. They were constantly working against me, and I felt like I would never measure up or fit in no matter how hard I tried. I kept coming up short. I found it a difficult challenge to figure out what was going on in my life, why this was all happening to me, and what I had done wrong to deserve it.

When people have not had their emotional needs met for a really long time, it affects their mental stability. It affects the ability to think clearly. There is a difference between emotions and feelings. Feelings run deeper than emotions and influence our thinking. Our emotions affect our nerves. Fear brings uncertainty, which creates instability, which affects our peace. It will require a new way of thinking differently, growing spiritually, and breaking off the debilitating limitations and patterns of fear, worry, and anxiety.

With all my heart, I want to help others struggling in this war so they can more easily identify and break up old foundations and patterns. The enemy relies on the lies and accusations deeply rooted in our emotional belief system. When you are young, the spirit of accusation plants lies and thoughts in your mind about who you are. You partner with that spirit when you give a false thought life and speak it out of your mouth. An example could be, "Nobody loves me." You then spend your whole life believing that lie. You partner with that spirit by believing it's true above what the Word of God says about His children. The enemy reinforces that lie through rejection and other situations.

He knows you very well. He is continually setting you up and working you over to wear you out. You rehearse the emotions from the event as if it just happened. Triggers are powerful because they often involve the senses. Places, things, sights, sounds, and especially smells have a profound effect on your memory. This elicits a response to get you to partner with him and keep the cycle alive. He will trigger something out of our subconscious and immediately a temptation comes to us. The enemy knows our thoughts affect our will. We become the product of our thinking. Therefore, it is important to pay attention to what you're thinking about and not come into agreement with what thoughts are from the enemy. Just keep in mind that God can bring you to breakthrough no matter how daunting the cycle seems. Be encouraged because Jesus has already defeated this demonic entity, so you cannot lose.

With all that said, let's briefly discuss what makes up a pattern. A pattern is defined as "a cycle of behavior, an acquired habit or learned behavior that repeats itself in a predictable way."[24] The definition of a cycle is "a series of events that are

---

24. "Pattern - Definition, Meaning & Synonyms." Vocabulary.com. Accessed March 20, 2022. https://www.vocabulary.com/dictionary/pattern.

regularly repeated in the same order."[25] The cycles of patterns if positive, move you forward. However, a similar cycle of patterns, if negative, will prevent any forward movement.

Are your choices destroying your life? Mine were. I allowed my anger and irrational behavior to affect my choices because my emotions ruled me. I was always in crisis. It took little to set me off, and the enemy was counting on that. It is vital for you to learn how to stand your ground against the lies of deception, to know who you are in Christ as a child of the Most High God. We must learn to not back down, always be alert, and aware of the enemies' tactics. Find your strength in the Lord and who He is and what He did for you on the cross. Take every thought captive that tries to exalt itself against your mind (2 Corinthians 10:5).

What hold does the enemy have on you from your childhood? As a child, the enemy weaves hatred into your life by planting the seeds of demonic destruction. Have these spirits created a false foundation of a demonic structure by creating a stronghold in your mind? The root system creates a stronghold in your mind combining a host of negative emotions and actions designed so that you fall to the enemy's deception.

God has a plan for your life that was written before you were born (*Jeremiah 1:5*). You must stay fixed on His plan. Stay on the narrow path to freedom however long it takes. The terrain might be unfamiliar, rough, and lonely. Be willing to move beyond what is comfortable and explore the new purposes He has

25. "Cycle - Definition, Meaning & Synonyms." Vocabulary.com. Accessed March 20, 2022. https://www.vocabulary.com/dictionary/cycle

for you. He will test your willingness to trust Him in new ways of thinking. A new love will spring forth in you, a new feeling that you have never felt before. You stay on the cross until He takes it from you. Don't be impatient. Stay until He heals you. Jesus Christ is the only One who can heal your heart. Stop looking for someone or something to bring healing.

Man cannot take the place of what only Christ can do in your broken state. That's what He did on the cross for you and me.

The blood that He shed at Calvary washes over your mind to heal the wounds and the pain in your heart. Your redemption only lies within Him. Ask Him to touch and heal the broken places of the past. In order for a change of heart to occur, the issues of the heart must be dealt with. Your attitude will change through that love encounter. All of a sudden, you will see oh how much He loves you. It takes great faith to face and overcome the giants from your past. Cry out to Him for His Spirit of truth. Seek His truth that sets you free. Your past abuses or abusers don't define you! Your spirit can be at war in your mind and heart because of past perspectives and false truths. Your thoughts can negate where you are going. New cycles and thought patterns must be created.

Remember, sometimes the truth hurts, but it is the only way to freedom. Accept that there is work in your inner man that needs to be done. There is a deep healing that must take place in the Jezebel afflicted soul. Healing begins with recognizing, repenting, and renouncing. Do not fight that fact. Everyone needs help in their broken state. If you do not think you do, sorry friend, but that's pride. Pride is the enemy's number one tactic to keep you stuck. Pride is a snare of the enemy to keep you stuck in your past cycles. Pride will tighten the enemy's hold on you by continually reminding you of past betrayals, failures, regrets and then he heaps guilt, shame, and condemnation on your head. Denial, refusing to see what's in front of you, and quarreling with your Maker because you always want to be right only keeps you trapped and unwilling to let go of things you should have let go of a long time ago.

No one is perfect on this side of Heaven except Jesus. We cannot remain blind and unaware. We sin in ways that don't line up with the Word of God. Do not blame others for where you are. This only prolongs your process. Take responsibility for your sin and shortcomings. It will take determination to break the years of torment the enemy has created in your mind. Take inventory of your heart's motives and be honest about your spiritual condition. When you become despondent because your emotional state is numb and lifeless, you're less likely to change your situation. Don't allow the enemy to steal your identity in Christ through self-pity and self-loathing.

Through trauma and abuse, I had become a victim. I suffered from a victim's mentality, which kept me in self-pity. This is a sin because that is not our identity in Christ and what He died to give us. Becoming a victim is the biggest stronghold the enemy creates in your mind throughout your life because he knows it keeps you in sin and deception. You must be willing, teachable, and remain diligent in seeking the face of Jesus. Push through the really hard times when you do not understand what the Lord is trying to show you.

I found that journaling really helped during this time. Writing everything down will help you have a clearer picture of what you are dealing with. The Holy Spirit was speaking to me continually about the cycle I was in. It took me many years to realize what He was saying. He would reveal the next step through prophetic revelation. It came through dreams, scriptures, songs, prophetic words, and people. That is why journaling is so important. My revelation always came in parts. I would have to go back and reflect on my journal to see everything the Holy Spirit was saying to me and how it would always fit together. One puzzle piece at a time. I discovered that this is how he brings revelation to break generational curses. That is why everything you hear, discern, or see is so important.

One thing for sure, journaling would always bring to light another area of my flesh that had to die or another part of my heart that needed to be healed. Another curse I was living under, of course, one I did not know was there. The cycle of Jezebel's attacks is a demonic fortress of lies that must be destroyed. This demonic spirit spins an intricate web of lies like a spiderweb to ensnare you. It creates a stronghold of mind control through establishing a false belief system of lies that capitalizes on physical, emotional, and mental trauma in your life. It also works with tying up your emotions so deeply that you just believe it is part of life. When you accept and embrace these lies, they affect your attitudes, emotions, behaviors, and you become entrapped and ensnared through the false identity that has been created. This principality is compiling evidence in your life to build a firm foundation. He builds an illusion that he wants you to believe. The more lies he can get you to believe, the stronger his foundation will be. He then takes the evidence he gathers and accuses you before God. Then he uses your sin cycles and generational sin cycles against you. In the next section, I want to share with you how the Holy Spirt helped me to identify these negative repetitive cycles. As you partner with the Holy Spirit, you will gain the knowledge and wisdom to walk in your freedom and experience His great love.

Satan knows that if he can influence the thoughts of your mind, he can control you. If these thoughts remain, they become a stronghold in your life. As the enemy plots to gain control and power over your mind, he is creating a false delusion of who God is. He creates doubt and unbelief that make you question everything about God and who He is. The greatest deception comes to challenge your faith, to steal and rob you of your faith and your joy. He uses this deception to keep you in the false identity of his creation. God will light up your destiny and awaken all that He has for you by breaking up the enemy's control over humanity.

The enemy takes your greatest assets in God and perverts them in order to make it look like your greatest struggle.

For instance, my greatest asset is to be a freedom fighter, a mighty, valiant, warrior for God. The enemy used anger and hatred to get me to fight everything and everyone in life except the real spiritual enemy of my soul. In order to be free, you must accept where you are and that you need God's help! Take inventory of your inner thoughts, emotions, motives, attitudes, prejudices, addictions, habits, and hidden sin. Master the unknown to be a conqueror!

I have noticed that so many people are finding themselves walking in the realm of unbelief, ignorance, and darkness. Tattered, beaten up, and paralyzed by the enemy with no will to fight anymore. They feel unwanted, unworthy, unneeded, unsuccessful, and hopeless, tossed on the rubbish heap of history, searching for a place to belong. Doubting whether God is real and worth the decision they made to accept Jesus Christ, and completely unaware of their position as a child of God. Satan has clouded their spiritual eyes and perception, resulting in faulty heart receptors, causing their heart to become cold and dead. Because of this continual onslaught of adversity and warfare, people are losing hope.

EVIL FOREBODING

A place of brokenness, coupled with a victim mindset keeps you in self-pity with murmuring and complaining. The place where you're only surviving in life, just going through the motions, hoping to one day hit the mark. Oh, how I remember that place, being in a constant state of emotional turmoil, with highs and low lows, and daily mental trauma. I would fight evil foreboding thoughts, triggers, fears, worry, and anxiety. It causes you to doubt the God you serve, His love, and tender mercies for your life. Doubting your worth before God, you feel you're not good enough and unlovable because of your past sins. Every day the enemy has flogged your mind with thoughts of what could happen, would happen, and should happen. You find that you are always asking yourself if this onslaught will ever stop, or if you're ever going to get free?

When I came to Christ, I remember these attacks were ferocious and debilitating. Its like you have some sort of vice on your head and a wet blanket thrown over your soul. It weighs you down. I was lifeless, with a dead heart and a severed will. He persecutes the poor of heart (*Psalm 10:2*) with tremendous pressure to keep them bound and in great distress; wanting nothing more than for them to give up. I was experiencing things such as lost promises, dreams, gifts, hopes, and treasures, hooked with fetters and chains as a prisoner. I was trying to fight to get free from the hidden bonds of sin and wickedness.

Are you fighting so desperately for freedom that you don't care anymore how you get it? You don't care who you have to push down, step on, or step over along the way. You just want to advance on the journey so badly that you are totally unaware of the grip that slander, jealousy, competition and envy have in your heart. Are you operating in the realm of the soul instead of the spirit, unconsecrated to God? The enemy will use pride to make you believe other Christians don't deserve to move ahead of you. God's Kingdom is not like this world.

Matthew 20:26-28 (AMPC)

26 Not so shall it be among you; but whoever wishes to be great among you must be your servant,

27 And whoever desires to be first among you must be your slave—

28 Just as the Son of Man came not to be waited on but to serve, and to give His life as a ransom for many [the price paid to set them free].

Satan's hidden agenda is to keep you trapped in his strongholds and schemes, to fulfill his plan and strategy based on the lies he wants you to believe. These tactics become patterns and cycles of sin and emotional behaviors. That is how he maintains the grip he has on you, and how he keeps you in the pit of despair. Have you ever found yourself in a wicked ambush by the enemy? He uses his strength, opposition, and torment to keep you caught in that cycle. Every time you get up and try to move ahead or advance, the enemy comes out of nowhere with a fierce attack to pounce on you and knock you back down, oppress and devour you. You then remain stuck and stay wounded in the same repetitive cycle of torment, wondering where God is. Why is God allowing this to happen? What am I learning in this situation?

This is exactly where I was until the Holy Spirit gave me a dream. I was riding a bike on a road. As I was peddling along, I could see the same debris on the road. I would make a turn and I would peddle up the same hill with the same trash on the road. In the dream, I would think that I already went this way, but I would continue to make the same turns only to find myself in the same place over and over. I recognized these patterns and cycles in my choices in my relationships with others. I would notice the same fighting cycles with my husband, almost step by step, repeating one after another. The Holy Spirit began speaking to me about the choices I made that were reoccurring and destructive. He taught me to make a different choice when situations would occur. I had to learn to walk in the spirit instead of my flesh because my flesh was clearly dominating my life. That was the root of so many of my problems.

My emotions would rule over me time and time again, and I would get caught up in fighting the wrong battle in the flesh. As long as we live on the earth, we will be engaged in a war. This isn't a physical war, but a spiritual war, and your mind is the biggest battlefield. The enemy wants you to believe that it is the people in your life that are continually fighting against you for no reason at all. Your loved ones are not off limits to him. He doesn't care who he uses. If he can get you fighting the people in your life, then he distracts you from fighting him with your spiritual weapons. The most important thing is to stay engaged at all times. I would get a little relief from the warfare and then I would rest and drop my guard and "BAM!" Here he would come again. I would be unprepared because my focus and attention had shifted off of prayer and the Word of God. He will attack you and try to get you to sin right before your breakthrough because he knows he can steal it away from you when you sin and partner with him. He played on my emotional triggers to trip me up every time until the Holy Spirit revealed what was happening. If you ask Him, He will show you because He wants you to live in the freedom Jesus died to give you.

"Be alert and of sober mind. Your enemy the devil prowls around like a roaring lion looking for someone to devour (1 Peter 5:8, NIV)."

"Fight the good fight of the faith. Take hold of the eternal life to which you were called when you made your good confession in the presence of many witnesses (1 Timothy 6:12, NIV)."

When we war against the enemy, he wages war against us any way he can. Some refer to this as spiritual backlash. The enemy will walk through any door that we have opened. Our experiences train us, by the power of the Holy Spirit, to be on spiritual high-alert. Anything we do for the Lord, whether it be witnessing, deliverance, or healing ministry: the enemy will come in to retaliate against us. He tries to punish you for walking in your destiny. He knows when you have been through a lot in your life, it doesn't take much to get you to cower down and give up. The enemy uses fear and intimidation to get you out of your spiritual position.

The first signs of worry, stress, anxiety, fretting and evil foreboding begin with a thought. It should be a red flag that we are operating in the wrong realm. Believing the lie opens a legal door for the attack because it is contrary to the Word of God. Pay attention to what you are thinking. You must take that initial thought captive and expose it for the lie it is. The devil is a liar. He plants lies in your mind to take over your thoughts. These racing lies come flooding in to keep you in confusion. Confusion does not come from God. It comes from the demonic realm (1 Corinthians 14:33). His main ploy is to destroy your joy and faith, so you will doubt who God is. Your faith will allow you to do great exploits for God.

He will use the people in your life, usually the people you love and care about the most. He leaves you so wounded that every time you start feeling strengthened, he will attempt to instill fear or intimidation in order to get you to cower back down again. The enemy is using every negative thought to paralyze you on this road to Glory. He gets you on the run and then you begin to operate out of the wrong spirit. You switch loyalties operating from a defeated position that you are not even aware of. You misplace your faith and fall back to your old ways, which are not God's ways. Before you know it, you are fighting in your own strength, always a defeated position, making your flesh your idol and your god. The enemy sees you as you see yourself. He is aware when you don't know how to fight, and he takes full advantage.

Believers and unbelievers alike are in a place where spiritual truths become hidden. There is power in spiritual truth, and the enemy knows it. The light of heaven is a spiritual truth which has the power of faith. Therefore, if there is no truth, faith becomes blinded in thick darkness. The condition of the human soul and spirit greatly interests the enemy. The enemy is developing new falsehoods in opposition to the truth, blinding humanity's eyes. God is warning and revealing the conditions of the heart of humanity.

The god of this world has been strategically planning the takeover of the minds of humanity. *In 2 Corinthians 4:4 KJV, "In whom the god of this world hath blinded the minds of them which believe not, lest the light of the glorious gospel of Christ, who is the image of God, should shine unto them. "* The god of this world has blinded the minds of those that do not believe. The spirit of unbelief affects and veils our belief and trust in God. This is the same spirit that hindered the disciples from casting the demons out of the demoniac boy in (*Matthew 17:20).* Satan wants to control the minds of the inhabitants of the world so that he can force them to worship him.

Besides the deceptions and shame heaped upon humanity, the lust for power is a common spiritual temptation. The easiest road to power is through a false sense of control. The enemy uses many forms of control, but witchcraft has its own aspect in mind control to steal the souls of men. It causes blockages that prevent one from beholding the glorious light of the Gospel of Christ. If Satan gets in our minds, then he has the entire person. Glory to our Lord and Savior Jesus Christ, who through His magnificent wisdom, has provided apostolic prayer strategies and weaponry through His Word to destroy the forces of darkness. Let us dig deeper into this attack.

We see in *2 Corinthians 3:13-14 NKJV, "... unlike Moses, who put a veil over his face so the children of Israel could not look steadily at the end of what was passing away. But their minds were blinded. until this day the same veil remains uplifted in the reading of the Old Testament because the veil is taken away in Christ. "* There is an intense end time release of mind control against the nations. Just as there are drugs strategically being released in the end times, so goes the spirit of mind control. We are the gate keepers of our mind. What you don't take authority over in your thoughts will continue to control you.

Don't be deceived by these ominous evil spirits (*Psalm 10:8*) bringing destruction upon your life. These wicked spirits sit lurking in the shadows just waiting for the perfect opportunity to murder the innocent who are unaware. Satan is the tempter; he continues to lure people into sin (*1 Peter 5:8*). Sin is lawlessness (*1 John 3:4*) or the transgression of God's will, either by omitting to do what God's laws require or by doing what it forbids (*James 4:17*).

The transgression can occur in thought (*1 John 3:15*), word (*Matthew 5:22*) or deed (*Romans 1:32*). Since God demands righteousness, sin is defined in terms of humanity's relationship. Sin is thus the faithless rebellion of creatures against the just authority of their creator. Sin is rebellion against God's law, the standard of righteousness. (*Psalm 119:160*) Violation of the law of God in thought, word, or deed shows the sinfulness of a human heart. Sin is a contradiction to the holiness of God's image mankind bears. Sin is the death of the soul. A man dead in trespasses and sins has no desire for spiritual pleasures. A lost, fallen, or dead spirit of a man is a state of conformity to this fallen world we live in.

Satan is the author of the proud and ungodly, and rules in the hearts of disobedience. Through rebellion and disobedience, they become his prisoners. It is a sad and terrible description of which has gripped the hearts of humanity but who can remove himself out of it, in his own strength, through dead works? Dead works leave you empty and exhausted with no results. Reflect upon the emotional misery of a person, shown in their deplorable state by nature, separated from God, cut off from the body of Christ, fallen from the covenant promise, having no hope, and no promise for the future.

"Christ and His covenant are the foundation of all Christian hope. Salvation is far from the sinner, but God is a help at hand to His people; And this is all by the sufferings and the death of Jesus Christ. God's eternal love or good-will toward His creatures is the fountain whence all His mercies flow to us; And that love of God is a great love, and that mercy is rich mercy. And every converted sinner is a saved sinner; delivered from sin and wrath. The grace that saves is free, undeserved goodness and favor of God; And He saves, not by the works of the law, but through faith in Jesus Christ. Grace in the soul is a new life in the soul. A regenerated sinner becomes a living soul, he lives a life of holiness, being born of God: he lives, being delivered from guilt of sin by the pardoning and justifying grace. Sinners rolled themselves in the dust, a sanctified soul sits in heavenly places, are raised above this world by Christ grace. The goodness of God in converting and saving sinners heretofore, encourages others in the after time, to hope in His grace and mercy. Our faith, conversation, and eternal salvation are not of works, least any man should boast. These things are not brought to pass by anything done by us, therefore all boasting is shut out. And this is all a gift from God and the effect of being quickened by His power. It was His purpose to which He prepared us by blessing us with the knowledge of His will and His Holy Spirit producing such change in us, that we should glorify God by our good conversation and perseverance to holiness." (Matthew Henry Concise Commentary on the Bible)

It is impossible to carry the Glory of God with unrepented sin in your life. We must strive for holiness but rest in grace. Are there holes left in your soul from being wounded that you refuse to let go of and do things God's way? The enemy uses cycles of bitterness and offense to have an open door to enter and attack you with sickness and pain in your body. So many think that sickness is their cross to bear, and that is a lie from the pit of hell. Through His mercy, God will use sickness and suffering to sanctify us and pull us into a relationship with Him. The enemy makes you believe that you have done something wrong to deserve it. We must recognize who is at work with this deception. Usually, right before your breakthrough, the enemy sets you up using another person in your surroundings to offend you. Once you allow that bitterness to take root, you become angry, and the enemy feeds off of your anger to keep you in sin. Once you are in unforgiveness and sin, he has an open door to put sickness on you. Most of the time, we just take what the enemy dishes out because we don't know who we are in Christ or the authority we have in Him. We do not have to settle for everything the enemy dishes out.

It's in our darkest hour that it seems so hard to breathe, when you feel nothing but the pain, fear, heaviness, and oppression that has grabbed hold of you. It's all on your chest, pressing down on you. The pressures and weights of the world come crashing down. Everything that you have ever known is gone, leaving you wondering if you're all alone. God is raising the broken to life in this hour, giving them beauty for ashes. He will redeem and restore all (Isaiah 61:3).

Jezebel has to be repented for. Jesus gives you a chance for repentance. The unction of the Spirit of God is drawing you from the inside out. Don't ignore that which is calling you upward. Let hope arise. Let your defeated enemy know that darkness has to flee. You are a light and light shall disperse all darkness that the enemy has on you. All of Heaven is fighting for you. Don't remain in unbelief. Nobody can do it for you. Hope arises out of your ashes and the prison walls fall. When the enemy comes in like a flood, the Lord raises up a standard against him. He is calling all of His children to battle. I hear the Lord say, "Arise sons and daughters! Arise, all of heaven is with you, my deliverers."

The enemy speaks into our minds with accusations through our words. Our words are at the center of our warfare. He tempts you with words, thoughts, and pictures. There's power in the words you speak. (*Matthew 12:36-37)* warns that we are accountable for the words we speak. One word from God swallows up the words of the enemy by the Word of truth. God's truth destroys every lie. However, repeating the words of the enemy brings us into agreement with the enemy's atmosphere of lies.

Our words should produce and create confidence, hope, and not fear. The enemy gains control over us through the atmosphere of lies. He manipulates our emotions with lies to gain ground. We must condemn every strategic plan of the enemy. We must take authority and allow no weapon to be formed against us (*Isaiah 54:17*). We must decree the Word of God out loud. We must decree our victory. Decree God's will. We must decree words of blessing over our lives and those we love instead of cursing their lives. As God exposes the enemy, the enemy has to repay you double for your trouble. There is no demon that can curse you unless you give it the legal ground. We must be a people of faith and trust in God. Unfortunately, there are more people creating a world of lies from the enemy out of their mouths instead of declaring the truth out of their mouths that represents God's Word. We must get established in the Word of God and let it flow through us. Let it be our faith confession.

Fear is a spirit that comes in through an open spiritual door in a person's life. It can also come in through generational curses that comes in a bloodline from circumstances or some traumatic event that happens in a person's life. Some examples are unexpected death, divorce, serious sickness, mental illness, physical, or verbal abuse. When that person partners with fear instead of taking authority, repenting, and commanding it to leave, it just continues creating more mind battles. As a result, it keeps the person trapped in evil foreboding, always thinking or speaking that something bad will happen. I want you to understand, no matter what is going on in your life, your ultimate choice must be to trust God. Whenever you partner with fear you are only allowing it to continue. The curse will continue in the bloodline until someone takes a stand against it and breaks it off by recognizing it, repenting, and renouncing it by the power of the blood of Jesus Christ. It is a sin to live in constant fear. The Bible commands us not to be afraid. "Do not fear..." is in the Bible 365 times; once for every day of the year!

Being afraid gives the fear a legal right to stay in the bloodline. The curse passed through the birth canal when a baby is born from one generation to another generation. Why do you think "Do not fear..." is in the Bible so many times? Because God knew that the enemy uses fear against His children to make them afraid and use it to keep control of us. We then become His slaves. As the fear continues, we believe the lie, that it will never leave. The lies we believe about fear, stress, and worry only allow the fear to increase. Growing up, I thought of fear, stress and anxiety as a way of life. I believed it was a normal way of life because of my lack of knowledge of the truth in God's Word. I was never taught that Jesus had already won the victory over every plot the enemy sent my way. Jesus isn't worried or afraid, He already paid the price and defeated the enemy, so we could have peace and experience the Father's true love. He speaks His heart about this many times in the Bible. Consider that when your circumstances aren't changing, the cause may be that there is something in you that God wants to heal. He allows those same circumstances to come back around in order to bring them to light and heal you. Pay attention to the things you pass, going around the same mountain over and over. They are a tell tale sign something is there to pray about. Ask the Holy Spirit to bring revelation of it, and trust that He will show you in faith. You can't overcome that of which you aren't aware. Once you recognize what is in operation against you, immediately take authority over it. This is how God severs the cords.

There is no fear in love [dread does not exist]. But perfect (complete, full-grown) love drives out fear, because fear involves [the expectation of divine] punishment, so the one who is afraid [of God's judgment] is not perfected in love [has not grown into a sufficient understanding of God's love] (1 John 4:18 AMP). Those in this paralyzed state are lacking the knowledge of God's love. Mental and emotional torment can become crippling. Fear is a tormenter. It ravages the soul it overtakes. A fortress of generational fear through unforgiveness is the number one reason people find themselves overtaken by fear. In order to overcome fear, we must remain on the altar and allow God to uncover everything hidden deep within our hearts. We must let Him expose every curse, lie, bondage, and stronghold within us. We must choose to trust Him. It's not about your feelings or emotions. It's about your actions and your ability to choose to trust God and consecrate all fear to Him.

When you find yourself in the storm of fear and your answers seem far away, remember your world's not falling apart. It's falling into place. If your eyes are on the storm, then you fear, dread, and doubt the outcome. When your eyes are on the cross, and the One you know, then you will always know victory. The cross is the confidence we need. We can't fail if we keep pressing. So lift your hands, head, and eyes to the One who calms the storm because there is where your help, peace, and rest come from. You must choose the path of peace and rest.

Times of crisis require great strength in Him. There is no greater strength than faith in the light at the end of your tunnel. When we doubt God, we waste time. Instead of spending your time spinning in circles in your own head, take the time to remember who is on your side. We encourage steadfast faith by reviewing the triumphant experiences of those who went before us.

As a very troubled individual, my life was spiraling out of control because fear had gripped my heart from childhood. Never allow the enemy to make you a prisoner of war because of your past. Your past is just a stepping stone, not a life sentence of torment.

The enemy only has the power to suggest and try to convince you of something. If he had any real power, he wouldn't have to lie and deceive you into believing him.

If he can get you to doubt God, then he can use doubt and unbelief to send you racing into fleeting thoughts of evil foreboding, doom, and gloom. The enemy wants you to doubt the future and the goodness of God working in your life.

These racing thoughts get us in a constant state of trying to figure it all out. We then become paralyzed by analyzing and questioning God. We are so focused on the "why" instead of on the "who." Doubting gives you more questions and no answers. Jesus is the only One who has answers! He is the answer. In desperation, people will play mind games to keep control. They will try endlessly to control and manipulate those in their lives out of fear. All the decisions and choices in our lives are based on doubt and fear or out of truth. There is no middle ground. Faith is an established conviction concerning the things unseen and the settled acceptance of our future reward and peace. When we are controlling out of fear, we have left our position in Christ and have labored and fought in our own strength. We are fighting out of pride and vanity. People will use the silent treatment to control and manipulate. They will also use self-pity to get others to feel sorry for them and respond favorably to them so that they can feel loved and appreciated.

There are no boundaries to self-protection for the person controlled by fear. One who is shattered will only care about what is happening to them. They will set up boundaries to escape or isolate and shut down. These boundaries kick into overdrive when they feel like they are losing control or can't get people and situations to change their desired outcome. The future remains unknown. Fear wants you to hold on tighter and tighter until you literally squeeze the breath out of the surrounding people. Out of fear, we manipulate others to either gain or keep control of our position at all costs. Either way, this futile attempt is very unhealthy for the controlling person and those controlled by using fear.

A lack of control in your circumstances is a great test for your flesh to die to fear and self. Honestly, until recently, I really didn't understand how deep the root of fear was within me. The Lord uses the enemy to bring forth that which is buried deep within us. Uprooting the spirit of fear was a tumultuous time. I found myself in an emotional and vulnerable state, trying to hold on to what I thought was stable. I was trying to self-protect by defending myself and my integrity as the events were unfolding before me, forgetting that God is my defender and protector. One of the biggest trick the enemy uses is to make us think that people are our adversaries.

There is only one adversary, the devil. He uses those who are weak and vulnerable to come against us. In an immature state, we believe that it's the people in our lives who are against us. When Jesus was hanging on the cross, he knew who His real adversary was and knew it was not the people who hung Him there. He knew the real enemy when He said, *"Father forgive them for, they know not what they do (Luke 23:34)."* As we grow spiritually, we become more Christ-like and are more easily able to recognize the good in people instead of blaming them for every challenge we face in our daily lives.

The enemy will continually draw us back into the same cycles and patterns of fear in order to keep or regain control of a certain area of our lives. I was desperately trying to keep my footing and choose to trust God. I lost my focus and my peace. The struggle was unbearable as I fell apart every other day. Something else would happen and I would be a mess again. I felt like I was falling short and failing the test. I was full of shame, guilt, and condemnation, never taking into consideration God's mercy and grace. I was trying to perform my trial perfectly. I have had significant trust issues my whole life because of all the betrayals that I have experienced. The enemy gets into the mind and soul of an individual and controls them with fear. When you allow fear to become all consuming, fear unintentionally becomes an idol.

We must take authority over every demonic attack against us and our children. Any attack of the enemy that we do not immediately take authority over gives Satan the legal ground against us to remain there. It is so important to take every thought captive that tries to exalt itself against the mind of Christ. We have the mind of Christ; therefore, we must not tolerate fear, stress or anxiety. The Word of God says, *"So do not fear, for I am with you; do not be dismayed, for I am your God. I will strengthen you and help you; I will uphold you with my righteous right hand (Isaiah 41:10, NIV)."*

Take comfort in knowing He is with you, helping you fight the battle. A lack of knowledge and truth in the Word creates a great disadvantage for all affected by this debilitating spirit. There are many levels of fear people experience. Panic is when a person is in constant fight or flight. This level of fear usually comes in through trauma in a person's life. Fear bombards the mind with all sorts of thoughts that end up keeping the person paralyzed in fear and panic.

The enemy will use the same tactic of fear against an individual if it works. They become unable to perform daily life. Social gatherings become difficult. Most people do not know what they are fighting. I didn't struggle with panic or panic attacks, but I have witnessed this firsthand. I suffered a lot of stress and anxiety, which would put me in flight, fright, or fight. Many times, I would just completely shut down because I could not figure out how to get free or get my situation to change. However, ignoring fear only gives it a stronger hold on you. The more complacent you are, the more areas of your life it takes. As a child of God, we are not a slave to the spirit of fear. We are called to overcome.

The key strategy of the enemy is to strike fear in the hearts of all humanity. His focus is to steal our peace, joy, hope, and faith. Most of all, our faith and trust in the Lord. This damages our perception of who God really is. Fear distorts the truth from what the Word of God says. Fear goes against everything God's Word says about His character. God created us in His image. If we don't know who He is, then it is impossible to know who we are according to His perspective and plan for our lives. The world shouts at us about who we are or who we are not according to the world's perspective. We look through the eyes of the past: past hurts, past failures, and past sins. Our filter becomes stained and blurry. Doubt and unbelief set in when we are constantly told who we should be, or who we shouldn't be. This puts us under a man-pleasing spirit in which we do everything we can so that we can feel accepted and not rejected.

"The Spirit himself testifies with our spirit that we are God's children —(Romans 8:16, NIV)."

The people who know God, not just casually but intimately, know that His relationship makes you strong. The enemy tries to make himself large and intimidating to you, just as Goliath did to Saul and the soldiers. He made accusations and yelled threats to mentally torment and paralyze the soldiers. Then along comes David, a man who knows his God, walking in faith. He knew his strength was in God. Goliath made all kinds of threats, but David stood unmoved because his courage came from the Lord. David's confidence and courage were evident as he stood before the giant.

The onslaught of lies from the enemy is to scare you into believing his lies. He roars and makes all the noise he can to terrify you. These tactics are used to get you to be afraid and partner with him. He tells you your situation is hopeless and will never change, so he can get you to confess these things out of your mouth. Everything he shouts at you is contrary to the truth about who you are in Christ as a child of God. God only gives His children the very best, and the enemy knows this. We are valuable to God. If your confession is about the negative stuff the enemy is doing, then where is your faith?

Lack of faith does not change your enemy. It changes you.

Lack of faith changes how you view yourself. The enemy knows when he has you fooled, and he continues to build off each lie you take as your own. Once deceived, you unwillingly entertain that spirit. Then you're trapped in the web; he knows shame flows from deception. You think the thought. You feel it is yours. You accept the guilt for the thought, and as soon as you do, he wins the battle. You immediately become trapped in that cycle because you aren't aware of the lie. The enemy just became a lot bigger in your mind. His strength just grew because you accepted all the negative reports. The evil reports of your health, finances, and family relationships that are in shambles.

Your kids aren't living for God, and so on. If you believe in the evil report you can't receive the blessings of the Lord.

Romans 15:6 KJV, "That you may with one mind (and) one mouth glorify God, even the Father of our Lord Jesus Christ."

James 4:7 KJV, "Submit yourselves therefore to God. Resist the devil, and he will flee from you."

Isaiah 26:3 KJV, "Thou wilt keep him in perfect peace, whose mind is stayed on thee: because he trusteth in thee."

Early in my salvation, I remember fighting strong opposition in my mind. My thoughts were continually racing and beating up on me. I would accuse myself and others in my mind. It was exhausting and emotionally draining. They kept me in continual emotional turmoil, not knowing what was going on. The enemy was accusing me in every area of my life. "You are not good enough. You can't do anything right. Nobody loves you. You're all alone. You will never be good enough. You are nobody. God will not forgive you because He does not love you. You are a sinner." Please understand that Satan and his demons have the power to put negative, false, and terrible thoughts in your mind and make them seem like they are your own thoughts.

There are many strongholds in the human mind that you must learn to take captive. Sexually perverted, ungodly thoughts will keep you in bondage and make you a slave to your sin when you act upon those thoughts. Fear, adultery, pornography, and sexual sin are all birthed in your thoughts first, and then acted upon. We become the thoughts we entertain. You can control your thoughts, even though the enemy makes you believe you do not. Though we exist in the flesh, we do not war in the flesh (2 Corinthians 10:4). The flesh is powerless against the wiles of the devil. It is God's power that destroys every stronghold and fortress built in our minds by the enemy. The enemy creates a cobweb of lies with your thought process, creating worldly views. Unfortunately, our lives reflect how many of these false truths we believe, revealing our lack of faith and trust in God.

The spirit of faith addresses the cast-down soul that has put his eyes on their circumstances and puts them back on God. When we walk in and obey the Holy Spirit, He reveals everything that is holding us back from a greater relationship with God. A greater relationship with Christ is where we find rest, peace, and hope. We must engage in the battle for truth and freedom. We do that by rightly dividing the Word of truth, taking every thought captive, and trusting God.

The onslaught of lies and accusations are attempts to undermine your authority and character in Christ. This spiritual warfare is a tactic of the enemy; he will use other people to strengthen your distress and oppression. He creates lies about you, so other people will come against you and cause you to doubt your identity and purpose in Christ. If he can get you to doubt who you are in Christ with the onslaught of lies and accusations, he can cause you to withdraw and feel you are always defeated. You become his slave and begin serving the wrong master. When you allow this, you become trapped and find it nearly impossible to escape, so you want to stop moving forward and give up.

You get caught up in the repetitive cycle of lies that you believe about yourself instead of the Holy Spirit who is pushing you to grow in the knowledge of who you are in Christ Jesus, and the knowledge of the sacrifice He made for you. We must repent for getting caught and ensnared by the enemy and making him what we fear instead of fearing God. Jesus silences the accuser and tears down the house of lies the enemy has built up in your mind. Stay engaged in the battle to get this freedom. This is an exceedingly difficult season where you must take captive every thought. You will recognize the lies you have been believing in learning the truth. You will find the truth in the Word of God. The Word of God reveals the true character of who God is and who He created you to be.

Gods' truth is greater than any lie and will always prevail against all the deception the enemy wants you to believe. Truth is the opposite of a lie. The battle for truth is in your mind, what you hear and believe about yourself. The spirit of accusation is constantly accusing you in your mind, one thought after the other. It will accuse and torment you day and night. You will overcome by taking every thought captive. Your thoughts govern your heart and what you speak about yourself and other people. Your mouth is the launching pad for truth and freedom. What you speak matters. Speaking the truth of the Word of God (the Bible) renews your mind and teaches you what God thinks of you instead of what the enemy. says Murmuring and complaining will only keep you in the pit. What is your perspective in battle? Do you see yourself as a victim or a warrior? Your perspective is everything when you are under attack and being assaulted. What lens are you looking from? When everything is cloudy, you cannot see clearly. When you feel defeated, you are weary and want to give up.

Let the challenges of life push us toward total dependence on you, Lord, as we surrender our will and run this race to accomplish the Lord's plans. I trust that taking up our cross and laying down our lives for each other will lead to an amazing life. Teach us to not be selfish or independent with your moment-by-moment leadership. We will finish this race.

HELP ME GOD

"On the contrary: If your enemy is hungry, feed him; if he is thirsty, give him something to drink. In doing this, you will heap burning coals on his head. Do not be overcome by evil, but overcome evil with good —(Romans 12:20–21, NIV)."

We must come to the end of ourselves and realize the battle belongs to the Lord. Once we surrender it all to God, He will fight for us. He will bring it all around full circle. If you keep your heart right, He will fight for you and you will overcome.

PERSECUTION

The greatest example in the Bible of character defamation was Jesus Christ. He endured persecution and demonization of who he really is. The enemy used people to deface his credibility as the Son of God. In *(John 13:21-27)*, Judas Iscariot betrayed Jesus, a most trusted disciple, later known for cowardice and treachery. Whatever Judas' motives, he led soldiers to the Garden of Gethsemane, where he identified Jesus by kissing him and calling him Rabbi (*Mark 14:44-46*). According to the Gospel of *Matthew 27:3-5*, Judas immediately regretted his actions and returned the silver to Jewish authorities, saying, "I have sinned by betraying innocent blood."

CHARACTER ASSASSINATION

When we find ourselves in various trials of betrayal, character assassination, or persecution, don't be alarmed because Jesus shows us how to respond to all of it. The Bible says that the Lord will vindicate us. We must keep our hearts right before God and allow Him to fight the battle for us. The Bible teaches us in *Romans 12:17 NIV, "Do not repay anyone evil for evil. Be careful to do what is right in the eyes of everyone."* And again in *Matthew 5:10 NIV, "Blessed are those who are persecuted because of righteousness for theirs is the kingdom of heaven."*

As a prophet of God, it is easy to be misunderstood your entire life because of the spiritual gifts you possess. Your own parents may not even understand who God has made you to be. In their lack of understanding and knowledge, they may even try to discourage you from what the spirit of God is telling you to do. When you have the gift of discernment, you can discern the atmosphere, demonic spirits in operation, but most importantly, the voice of God and all that is holy, including angels.[26] Remember, our battles are not for the temporary, but for the

---

26. GotQuestions.org. "Home." GotQuestions.org, August 27, 2015. https://www.gotquestions.org/gift-discerning-spirits.html.

eternal transformation of our souls. Paul never minimizes suffering but he insists with absolute conviction that future rewards will outweigh all present sufferings. We are learning discipline and endurance.

Romans 8:18 (NIV), "I consider that our present sufferings are not worth comparing with the glory that will be revealed in us."

Are you familiar with evil foreboding? Most people experience it and never really realize or understand what is happening. A New Thing Ministries makes a fantastic attempt at describing these feelings of impending doom. Forebodings are a constant irritation, the crippling sound of what if's and the dread of waiting. Fear, anxiety and dread clinch our soul and hang over us through our thoughts when we entertain evil forebodings."[27]

Proverbs 15:15 (AMP), "All the days of the desponding and afflicted are made evil by anxious thoughts and forebodings, but he who has a glad heart has a continual feast regardless of circumstances."

I would like to give you a life example of evil foreboding. My husband does construction, so our income has always fluctuated and at times, it was very hard. It always seemed no matter how hard we worked, we would just come up short. Many times, we didn't have enough to make ends meet. I was always terrified during the winter months. Christmas was always heartbreaking because we never had enough. I had learned to dread wintertime and Christmas. The fall season would be the time when I would

---

27. Fran O'Donnell says, "Evil Forebodings," A New Thing Ministries, March 26, 2020, https://anewthingministries.com/evil-forebodings/.

begin to have bad thoughts about the winter. I got to where I couldn't care less whether I had Christmas because I didn't know if we would have money. I had a really poor attitude about it. I didn't even want to decorate because I would be so heavy and oppressed by it. I would speak these vain imaginations out of my mouth. Good things would never happen to me. My confession was always one of great dread. After many years of being afflicted by this kind of thinking, a dear friend told me what I was doing. I had become so accustomed to the fear and dread that I wasn't even aware that I was falling into the enemy's trap every year. Once I recognized what was happening and repented for my sins, it all changed. When the next year rolled around, I was careful to watch and listen to what was coming out of my mouth. I was so thankful to God for the breakthrough.

It is easy to fall prey to an unsuspecting enemy when our anxious thoughts betray us because of life's challenging and uncertain circumstances. A deeper fear dictates our response to that deeper emotion. This fear triggers a negative, irrational response, which triggers an emotionally unhealthy reaction. We then switch from trusting God to making decisions out of fear and self-protection in our own strength.

For example, when someone rejects, offends, deeply hurts, or betrays you, how will you respond? My initial response was almost never godly. It was almost always in the flesh. That had to be worked in me and through me over a process. My reaction was always a defensive one. They misunderstood me my entire life because of this flaw that was disguised by a hidden warrior spirit that was born to fight. I had to learn to yield those angry emotions at the right time and in the right spiritual way. The enemy is good at perverting your gift. Your first response, most likely, will be anger because you want to protect yourself. There are open wounds in your soul from the past. They tend to just build up layer by layer, betrayal after betrayal because we refuse to just let them go, but God can heal us.

We hold on to them out of unforgiveness, which is a sin. We often think we are doing the right thing by holding on to them because we are trying to justify and self-protect. Often, we retreat inward and withdraw from life. We allow the enemy to isolate us because it is easier to just ignore than take inventory of the triggers and pain we are experiencing. God allows circumstances to happen to us to reveal what we are spiritually lacking and what has a grip on our hearts. I had so much hurt and pride that He had to work out of my heart.

The continual hurt by family, friends, and even strangers only deepens the anger, which gets you deeper into hatred and pride. Have you ever stopped and asked why this is happening over and over? I can't even count how many times I've asked God that question. Sometimes it is more about you than the other person. I'm sure that is hard to swallow, but the Lord showed me time and time again to reflect upon my own life, my heart's intentions. I would say, "God, this is so unfair; I don't deserve this. They are lying and making false accusations." God would say, "Alena, I'm not talking about them. I am talking to you. What is in your heart?" Only God alone knows what is truly in your heart. You cannot hide anything from Him because He is all-knowing.

Blaming others shifts the focus off ourselves. Ask God what is in your heart that is an open door for the enemy to attack you over and over again in this way.

Don't fall into self-pity and remain the victim.

I would always pray, "Create a clean heart in me, oh Lord. Show me what's in my heart that is keeping me from you. What's holding me back from surrendering to you (*Psalm 139:23-24*)." I promise if you find yourself in this pattern or cycle, there is a hidden key (curse) God is trying to reveal and bring to your awareness. In my own life, I have discovered every hard circumstance is revealing some issue in my heart or generations.

Sure, the intentions and issues in a person's heart is what's doing the hurting, but there is also a person receiving the hurt. A person's actions and words reveal their heart, pain, and brokenness, but your responses and reactions to them reveal what is in your own heart. The enemy reminds you over and over of the deep wounds in your soul that are open and bleeding to keep you in the cycle of unforgiveness, bitterness and offense. The spirit of accusation will continually accuse that person in your thoughts, reminding you of everything they've done over and over to you. It bogs down your mind with distracting and overwhelming thoughts of retaliation. That spirit's major objective is to get you to come into agreement with the enemy about that person, so he can use you as a weapon against them. He will try to use you to reinforce that person's weaknesses and shortcomings. Your focus is consumed against them and how you can pay them back.

LETTING GO

What is God's perspective on this situation? His perspective will never be contrary to what is in the Word. Usually, the biggest sin of offense is pride. Pride wants you to think about yourself and what you deserve or don't deserve. We must humble ourselves and surrender to God's perspective and His plan to bring us to a breakthrough. God's heart and motives are pure. He works everything for our good. We must act intentionally to choose joy and the fruits of the spirit over the works of our flesh. We must place our own motives and intentions at His feet so that He can work for and in us to release past hurts. Letting go preceeds the breakthrough that's coming forth.

What do you need to let go of? You cannot carry the past with you into the future. You must let go of everything before the new thing can come forth. Our soul is like a watered garden. We must weed out the garden by breaking soul ties. A soul tie is a relationship with anyone that isn't based in God's love, holiness, and freedom, but by soulish or sinful qualities such as lust, manipulation, abuse, domination, pride, bitterness, performance, fear, deception, and laziness. Demons can operate in and deepen the bondage present in soul ties. Sexual soul ties are the most powerful. Our relationships, past and present, must fall under the Lordship of Jesus Christ, so our hearts are free to function in a godly and wholesome way with the people God places in our lives. Unhealthy soul ties exist with former spouses, current spouses (operating in control, domination, manipulation, throu gh fear, belittling, or criticism), and any sexual partner outside of marriage.

Lastly this includes parent/child relationships (rebellion, people pleasing for acceptance, judgments, control, always trying to fix everything, no boundaries) or any relationship dominated by sin. There are good soul ties such as marriage, business partners, family, or good friends. There are also negative or ungodly soul ties in a relationship that bring you into bondage, rob you of your will, or are harmful to you. Many people are involved in unhealthy relationships or have soul ties in their minds and emotions tied to past relationship hurts and wounds. Specifically, it's when a person has control or influence over another in an unhealthy way. [28]

To break unhealthy soul ties, you must forgive the person and choose to honor them. Speak out loud, "in the name of Jesus, I break this unhealthy soul tie with [insert name]. I choose to honor and respect them, but I consecrate my life to You God, and I choose to be led by You and to please You with my life and with my choices. I release this person to You and consecrate my relationship with them to You. I renounce and reject any spirit that has gained ground in my life through a soul tie with this person in the name of Jesus. As an act of my will, I choose to separate my soul from everything I gave to this person. Give back to me the part of my soul that I gave to them. Amen."

---

28. Lipscomb, Pamela. "What Is a Spiritual Soul Tie?" Spiritual Gifts Today, June 13, 2017. https://spiritualgiftstoday.com/what-is-a-soul-tie/.

Walk in ongoing forgiveness and unconditional love for them. Lay them at the feet of Jesus, and understand that only He can change them by His transforming grace from the inside. Claim them for the Lord and His Kingdom. Rejoice in His power and might to transform hearts.

You can choose not to let the triggers of hatred rule your heart. So, the next time you see the person(s) choose to see them as Christ sees them. Jesus loves this person and does not ignore or minimize this person's sin. Jesus will do what is right for that person. Focus on Jesus and the healing and freedom He has for this person and you! The Lord once told me in prayer, it's easy to love those who love you back. It's a test of the love of God to love those who are unlovable. A person's severed will causes an inability to let others in and return love, affection, and acceptance.

You must be vigilant in seeking the new strategies and truths you have planned for your anger triggers. The devil will continue to come back and attempt to get you to believe the lies attached to your triggers. We must continue to review God's truth. What does God say about this trigger? How does God want you to meet each need and desire you to overcome? The key issue is that you must continue to fill your mind and heart by putting His teachings into practice in your daily life.

You hold the key to your own freedom. You just have to open the prison gate.

"Forget the former things; do not dwell on the past. See, I am doing a new thing! Now it springs up; do you not perceive it? I am making a way in the wilderness and streams in the wasteland (Isaiah 43:18–19, NIV)."

See where you are, be honest with yourself. Where are you going? Are you stuck in the dry wastelands? Are you looking in the rear-view mirror? What is your perspective? Integrating the heart and mind can sometimes be a war. Are you living in the past more than the future? Is the past constantly coming out of your mouth? Are you rehearsing over and over your betrayals and past hurts as though they just happened? Letting go takes intention. Your thoughts will negate where you are going, or where you are staying stuck. Being and becoming who you are is on the way to where you are going. Make a commitment to embrace healing.

Is something missing? If you're missing something that means it existed. Restructure your mindset. God calls forward, calls upward, and calls us out. God will evoke, invoke, and provoke us and push us to the new thing. Israel was stuck in old ways of thinking. The mindset of the past was holding them back. Don't remember the things from the past. Stop repeating them over and over. Emotional, spiritual, and physical sorrow leads us inward, and shuts us off from those we love.

What is a trigger? It is a reminder of past trauma. The reminder causes a person to feel overwhelmed with fear, sadness, anxiety, or panic. It may cause someone to have flashbacks of the event. A flashback is a vivid, often negative memory that may appear without warning. It can cause one to relive or re-experience the traumatic event. They lose all track of their immediate surroundings and get caught up in the memories playing over in their mind.

The triggers: places, people, objects, smells, sounds, words, and yelling are by themselves harmless. But when we connect with them in our minds with the memories of past events, often coupled with false beliefs, we give them the power to take us down a path and re-experience the emotional damage in our lives. We relive the brokenness, pain, and heartache repeatedly. This can affect the ones we share our lives with that are the closest to us. These triggers can set off a chain of events that are very destructive and explosive in a person's life. In order to live in freedom and break the power of the trigger, we must be willing to evaluate and identify the triggers in our life. Take responsibility for your actions and shortcomings such as fear, anger, self-pity, and victim mentality. Start with the obvious ones: a painful experience, a failure, and all forms of abuse.

What does your path to freedom look like? God wants us free from all bondages and past triggers. Once you identify the trigger, you can identify how that trigger affects your life today. The abuse or betrayal may have happened years ago, but the emotional damage is still very real today. We can be in bondage to the traumas of our past, or the temptations that have overwhelmed us from the past. We can continue to be on an emotional roller-coaster, letting our emotions control our moods, thoughts, words, and actions. Your thoughts and your emotions are tied to each trigger. The trigger may have been born out of an event in your life that first exposed you to that trauma.

Each one of these events opened a door of experience in your life, and now the memory, the site, the smell becomes the trigger magnet in the present to pull you down a destructive path today. Every trigger also has false beliefs connected to it. These false beliefs give the trigger so much power in your life. The sound of a low-flying jet triggers the thought, "Maybe this is another plane about to crash. Terrorists are here again. I can't be safe anymore." All kinds of false beliefs are connected to the trigger that's affecting your life.

Another person can have a similar experience, but they do not have any of the same or current triggers as you do that relate to this event. In one sense, everyone is different, yet we all have triggers of one sort or another. If we are going to gain control over these triggers in our lives, we must identify what those triggers are and the false beliefs that we have attached to them.

What gives the triggered thoughts power in your life? Who gives the triggered thoughts power in your life? You do! Each trigger only has as much power as you give it. The more important question is, how will you respond to the trigger or the person? Will you let the trigger pull you down a destructive path, or will you choose a different response as you speak God's truth into it? Make a list of them and describe your typical response to them.

Try to gain an understanding of what happens before the trigger goes off in your life. Does this trigger usually happen at a certain time of day or night? Or when you are with a certain person? What is the setup? What puts you in that vulnerable position where you easily give in to the trigger? Take your finger off the trigger. Make it your goal to not respond the way you have in the past. Some triggers related to temptations in our lives have power because we have not stopped the activity.

There is either an emotional payoff or we are simply unwilling to give up the trigger completely. We like the power it gives us for self-protection and self-defense. If we are to find freedom from that trigger, we must willingly choose to turn away from the temptations that go along with it. You must think before you respond. Think about the consequences of the choices you are making. Make your choice according to your newly-learned truth in the Word about your situation.

You must attack the lies associated with the trigger by bringing God's Word and truth into the picture. You must find out what God says about this issue in your life and then make it a clear part of your thought process. You will expose the lie of the enemy with the truth in God's Word. You must make a choice to never go down this path again. There is power for you in your choosing God's way. You must make a list of triggers and then list God's truth about the triggers in your life, such as anger and fear. What does the Word of God say about that? Below is a list of examples of the lie and then the truth. You must choose a new response to the person and triggered memory of the past. This new response needs to be based on God's truth. When you choose to go down the sinful path, you will immediately feel God's conviction and you must repent of the sin. Ask God to forgive you for the repeated cycle and behavior.

When the enemy tempts you with the memory of that sin, (often with a flood of shame each time) confess the sin, repent, and ask God's forgiveness. Then replace it with the truth in God's Word. We must confess our sin because God is faithful, and He forgives it. It's in our pride and rebellion that we cannot repent of our sins: the negative thought, the lie or accusation triggers the emotion, which triggers another thought (evil foreboding, paralysis), the action, the fear, panic, doubt, and unbelief.

Being left behind triggers the emotions of abandonment.
- "I'm not good enough" triggers the rejection that nobody loves me.
- "I'm all alone" triggers the "why is this happening to me?" This question triggers the victim mindset, which triggers the self-pity.
- "I'm never going to overcome this," which triggers emotions of depression, oppression, and heaviness.

Guilt, shame, and condemnation weigh you down, which causes despair and hopelessness. You strive and work hard to be accepted and loved, which gets you into performance, leading to perfectionism. This makes you codependent on everyone.

What spirit is behind the lie the enemy is planting in your mind? In reality, it's the enemy. He is working through the wounds and brokenness from past trauma. Offense triggers emotions of anger. All anger is driven by fear and works to add hatred. Resentment occurs when the spirit of accusation bombards you with evil thoughts about a person. Negative thoughts of sabotage, revenge, backlash, self-sabotage, and destruction triggers rejection which causes isolation, loneliness, self-loathing, and self-hatred. A victim mindset will murmur and complain using word curses, vows, and judgements spreading the message of Jezebel.

SLANDER

This spirit uses intimidation to make you cower down and lose the will to fight back against the demonic realm. He uses dominating people in our lives to control us by making threats and accusations, to come against us so we will back down and give up. Gossip and slander are the work of witchcraft and Jezebel uses them to create fear by turning others against you and making you out to be the betrayer and the ultimate problem. Avoid being a messenger of Jezebel by not spreading her lies and slander. Intimidation causes fear and pressure, so we will shut up for fear of what's coming next. The enemy does not want us to keep pursuing the prophetic gifting that's been placed on our lives.

This bully spirit will use you to bully others. Don't allow it to use you as a destructive force against others because you feel superior to them.

The spirit of accusation will work against you and your loved ones. This spirit creates toxic mindsets in your thoughts. It will accuse you, using your thoughts about yourself and others by telling you how bad they are. In your mind, the enemy accuses you; about yourself, who you are, and who you are not. He exploits every weakness, reminding you of past mistakes and failures. He will tempt you to be in competition, jealous of others, and envious of them. The enemy reinforces your distrust by making you suspicious of everyone and everything. He steals your joy and peace. He creates overwhelming mental challenges to keep you in crisis and emotional distress. Fear is a great example of this. Once he gets you to believe the lie, then fear becomes bigger than your faith in God. You lose your focus on Jesus when you allow this bombardment of thoughts and lies to consume you.

He whispers lies about others: your parents, spouse, children, family, coworkers, and friends. As a result, you are constantly bringing up their weaknesses and failures. He causes you to judge, criticize, and blame others. He is good at keeping strife and contempt going to cause harm and disunity. Take off the mask and swallow your pride. Admit what you are trying to hide. Face and accept what's going on. Stop blaming others. Face your demons head on instead of stroking them. You may not think that other people see but more people see than you realize. "Vain imaginings" and "evil forebodings" are nothing more than lies from Satan, attempting to drag you away from the light and into his darkness.

"Repentance isn't about paying for our sins; that's what Christ did. It's about rethinking our actions. It's literally changing your mind.

Punishment doesn't do that. Punishment can create obedience but not a true change of heart. Our hearts are exactly what God wants. If you want to know how well punishment and shame work, just look at our country's penal system."[29]

"So if the Son sets you free, you will be free indeed (John 8:36, NIV)."

Our sin causes our external decay, but it's our root system from deep within that supports our outward growth. Some of my plants died due to decay and deterioration from insects and the heat one summer. The following year they returned because of the root system. The root system was still growing and maturing underneath the surface. It may seem as if nothing is changing on the outside, but it's the unseen growth taking place deep within our roots because we are planted firmly and grounded in Christ.

The enemy works to set you up, strategically placing time bombs on your path to trip you up. He sets you up, slowly and undetected to create a big fall in your life. He knows your weaknesses and what it will take to get you back into those same old ways of stinking thinking. The enemy creates circumstances

---

29.Evans, Richard Paul. The Road Home. Waterville, ME: Thorndike Press, a part of Gale, a Cengage Company, 2020.

in your life to fill you up with temptations. He sabotages your relationships to bring chaos and division. He will keep you in a constant state of distractions, turmoil, disappointment, and discouragement. He constantly tries to get you back into old behaviors and destructive cycles.

This destructive behavior is connected to why people can't stop being addicts and why many suffer from food allergies and digestive issues. They are trying to escape their reality and numb themselves. I recently saw this firsthand with a recovering drug addict. A relationship ended because the other person walked out. The abandonment and rejection of this relationship caused the recovering addict to question everything, including: "Where was God?" What were they to do now? They felt so alone. The rejection made them feel unlovable and unwanted. As they doubted their worth and value, sobriety seemed insignificant to them. All the ground they had gained just slipped away. In their hopelessness, they sought some old friends for comfort. Unfortunately, the old friends reacquainted them with their old drug habits. One thought led to one poor decision that led to their demise. The Lord put this person on my heart one day with the sense that they were using again. I called them and sure enough, they had. I could hear the self-pity and the victim's mindset in everything they said. We must guard against the enemy's tactics to pull us back into old patterns of sin. When you do not know the root cause of your inner suffering, that's what trips you up every time. It's almost impossible to get free without the help of the Holy Spirit bringing divine revelation.

My friend, Carlen, was constantly being attacked by the enemy in her mind. The enemy knew her parents died in an accident when she was three years old. This thought is what triggered her memories of abandonment at the age of 3. Her first thought with any situation was often, "I'm going to be left behind." This thought is what her memories of abandonment at the age of three brought back to her remembrance every time. It was a lie! Her parents hadn't abandoned her. They had died. It was a generational issue. The next thoughts and lies were, "Here we go again." These thoughts are what kept the victim mindset in operation.

CARLEN'S MIND BATTLE

The first thought was, "I'm going to be left behind," which is what triggered her memories of abandonment at the age of three. It was a lie! Her parents hadn't abandoned her. They had died. It's a generational issue affecting the entire bloodline. This is where the fear first came in. She was always fighting separation anxiety. She was unaware of its origins and the trauma she had endured. She suffered from so much anxiety that she began to think she was going to die. She would throw up from all the stress and fear. She did not know how to handle it. She just wanted to run away to escape it, but it never left her. It tormented her for the majority of her life.

The truth:

Psalms 27:5, Deuteronomy 31:6, Isaiah 41:10, Psalms 34:18

The next thoughts and lies are, "I'm not good enough. I'm unworthy. Nobody loves me. I'm all alone." These trigger the emotions and thoughts of rejection. She felt rejected by her parents leaving, even though she did not understand any of it. She felt like she was being punished for something.

The truth:

John 15:8, Romans 8:28, Psalms 41:7, John 1:11

The next thoughts and lies are, "Here we go again. It's all happening again. Why me? I can't hardly keep my head above water. Why is God allowing this? Why is this happening to me? I'm doing everything I know how to do." These thoughts trigger the victim mindset. She found out that the parents that raised her were not her biological parents. She felt betrayed and lied to even though she was too young to understand any of what happened.

The truth:
Daniel 11:35

The lie:
"I cannot overcome this hopelessness. I'm going to be stuck in this forever. I'm not able to overcome this situation."

These thoughts trigger emotions and thoughts of self-pity. You constantly feel sorry for yourself and look for others to feel sorry for you, as well. You can actually want pity from man more than you want your healing from God.

The truth:
John 16:33, Prov 3:5, Phil 4:8

The lie:
nothing ever changes.

This thought triggers oppression, depression, and heaviness.

The truth:
Duet. 31:8, Jer. 29:11, Matt 11:28, Phil 4:8

The lie:
You're feeling weighed down. You just want to give up. You don't want to go on. You don't want to keep engaged and fighting the enemy.

These feelings trigger despair and hopelessness.

The truth for feelings of despair:
2 Cor 4:8, Psalms 42:5, Psalms 18:6, Isaiah 61:3

The lie:
You work so hard in your own strength to be loved and accepted that you become a people pleaser, always trying to fit in and find your place. These feelings trigger emotions and thoughts of striving in your own strength, instead of resting and abiding in Him. You become full of guilt and shame because no matter how hard you try, you just can't seem to get it figured out.

The truth for feelings of hopelessness:
Psalms 40: 1-3, 2 Cor 1:1-3, Romans 5:8 Romans 8:35

The lie:
I have to work so hard to fit in. I have to be perfect. I have to be the best.

The truth is that you are performance oriented and a workacholic ever striving to achieve success and recognition. The spirit of competition pushes you more in order to achieve to be better than others, while jealousy and envy pushes you to put others down so you feel and look better to others. Forgive yourself for believing the lies caused by the self-hatred, man hating spirit, and woman hating spirit.

ALENA'S MIND BATTLE

The lies: When betrayal comes again, it triggers memories of past traumas and persecutions. It brings the emotions to the forefront of your mind. All of a sudden, it feels like a very familiar place. A place that you have been to before. Memories, images, word curses, vows, and flashbacks are taking over your mind. It's a place of overwhelming emotions and tears. Immediately you feel the rejection. You feel pushed into a tailspin, feeling unwanted and unloved. You fear abandonment because that's how it ended the last time. The thought of being left again is devastating and unbearable. At this moment, you realize the deep-rooted fear that still exists in your soul. Your desperate plea to God for help and your desire to be free of all the pain, heartache, and sorrow starts bubbling up and resurfaces, along with the emotions of the trauma.

A victim mindset will tell you, "Why is this happening to me? I did nothing to deserve this. Poor me. Why did God allow this to happen? God must not care about me, or He wouldn't allow people to do this to me." You then feel like you are up against the wall with no way out. You feel as though you are forced to deal with betrayal and persecution alone. You don't understand, so you just hide in isolation and silence for fear of anyone seeing the pain in your heart. You turn inward to protect yourself.

The more you think about it, the greater offense, bitterness and resentment grow. These are the forerunners of anger and hatred. You fear what is happening and it fuels these emotions.

As you ponder on your past and current situations, your anger builds to hatred for those who have hurt you. Your perception then becomes tainted, and the path just got darker. From this point, if you operate out of this realm, you are no longer operating from the Spirit of God. Hatred is the opposite of love and everything that is God.

A spirit of accusation immediately floods your mind with insult upon insult against you as a person and against those who hurt you. It tells you that you deserve what's happening because you are a horrible person, and the enemy reminds you of all your past mistakes. The person who hurt you will often work with this accusation to turn the tables from themselves to you in the hope you will fall for it again. The spin is to blame you for the betrayal and persecution.

Evil foreboding sets in as you think of fear and the worst-case scenario. You try to figure out if this really is your fault. Did you really deserve what happened? Is what they said the truth? What does the future hold? How will I make it? How will I survive again?

Retaliation is a way of wanting to self-protect. You feel you need to defend yourself and pull people on your side of the situation. You feel you need to get even with the person who hurt you.

Your thoughts lead to sabotage and revenge. What can I do to pay them back what they deserve? You just want to get even.

By the time you get to this point, your flesh is over your spirit, and you have lost the voice of the Holy Spirit because it has become faint while trying to pass through your flesh that wants to be in control. Pride and rebellion set in, and you don't want to listen. You just want to be in control of everything you are feeling. Pride thinks you are right about everything. There is no reasoning with you at this point because the error of your ways blinds you. Rebellion wants you to prove you are right about everything. Rebellion wants you to throw out all that you know about Jesus, all your past victories, and all the ground you have gained. You refuse to submit to God's plan because you can't trust Him or anyone at this point. You just want vindication at all cost.

The choices you make will lead to reaping what you sow. Vows, judgements, and word curses start flowing from your mouth as you allow the enemy to gain control of your heart and soul; cursing others along with cursing yourself.

The truth: *"For there is nothing hidden that shall not be disclosed, nor anything secret that shall not be known and come out into the open (Luke 8:17, AMP)."*

Life can surely be a challenge! Do you find yourself under tremendous pressure? I know I am. When your heart is under fire, the Lord is refining you with His holy fire. The pressure and heat bring out the dross (impurities) in your heart. God's refinement reveals all the hidden impurities in your heart so that He can cut the strings that entangle you!

When you don't understand what is going on, you are at a disadvantage to the enemy. The enemy uses chaos and negative circumstances in our lives to create fear, doubt, and unbelief in our minds. The enemy wants to gain control of our hearts and emotions so he can control our every move. He is counting on your lack of trust in God in your situation. He wants you to doubt God's love for you. The enemy's plots and schemes against you are being revealed. Pay attention! God works all things together for the good (*Romans 8:28*). The enemy never stops looking for or creating opportunities to sabotage you. All sin is an open door for him to walk through and bring destruction. Make no mistake, he will continually set you up to fall into his same old trap. He uses the same triggers of sin, sex, lust, adultery, alcohol, drugs, unforgiveness, offense, self-pity, victim mindset, anger, and negative thoughts to ensnare you.

He knows how to set you up and how to exploit your weaknesses. He uses the same repetitive sin cycle against you until you recognize what he is doing and stop it. He then works them all together for his advantage by exposing them to others! He sets you up for a big fall! Sin may seem inviting, fun, secret, and even seductive, but it all has consequences. You can manipulate, lie, cheat, conceal encrypted messages, and whitewash conversations in order to continue in deception, but God knows! He is all-knowing. In His supremacy, He is omnipresent. He is everywhere you are. There is nothing you can hide from Him.

We must realize that there is always a dark agenda working against us through destructive games and manipulative thoughts that are being played out by the enemy in order to gain control our hearts, minds, will, and emotions. Do not allow the enemy to drag you back into the same bondage that you have overcome. God does not give you the strength and courage to overcome for you to find yourself right back in the same old web of lies, manipulation, and entanglement. He warns of impending danger coming our way, but all too often, we are surprised, like we came around a corner and ran into a cobweb.

The Lord will give you warnings of what the enemy is plotting against you, but you have to be a watchman on the wall to discern what's coming. Almighty God is for you. The Lord will expose every evil plot and lie man has intended to harm you. The Lord will protect those who love Him. When the righteous cry out, He delivers them out of it all. No evil shall befall you. If you find yourself caught up in some destructive sin cycle, cry out to the Lord, He will set you free. Repentance is essential for your freedom. Don't keep allowing the thief, the enemy, to come in through your open door(s) to steal your life, marriage, family, joy, and peace! Amen!

The Holy Spirit was revealing to me the secret of having rest and peace in the difficult times of life. God is preparing an army that understands the battle. We are the vessels being prepared to bring Heaven to earth. It's not a physical battle, but a spiritual war between us and the unseen realm of darkness. The battle is in our minds, the warring for understanding. With warring comes authority and power. The enemy wars with us over receiving understanding because that is where he meets defeat. As the Holy Spirit pours out His Spirit upon all flesh (as prophesied in Joel and Acts), we understand our authority and power in Christ, which will defeat the enemy. We must seek an outpouring of the Holy Spirit, just as the disciples did in the upper room. We must expect an encounter that will bring the Kingdom of God to people. We must seek the Holy Spirit to empower us for great and mighty exploits in God's Kingdom.

It is so important that we do not dwell on the attacks of the enemy, which can elevate his position. Instead, we must focus on our relationship with God by going deeper into His Spirit. Jesus tells us, *"Yet a time is coming and has now come when the true worshipers will worship the Father in the Spirit and in truth, for they are the kind of worshipers the Father seeks. God is Spirit, and his worshipers must worship in the Spirit and in truth (John 4:23–24, NIV)."*

True worship has nothing to do with where we attend church, what songs we sing, which pastors or leaders we listen to, or whether we raise our hands or sit quietly. These are only external signs of worship.

True worship is internal and comes through our spirit communing with God's Spirit.

It can take place wherever we are... even all alone in our homes. This is where we find the strength to live the life that God desires for all born again believers in Christ Jesus! We are new creations!

"So from now on we regard no one from a worldly point of view. Though we once regarded Christ in this way, we do so no longer. Therefore, if anyone is in Christ, the new creation has come: The old has gone, the new is here (2 Corinthians 5:16–17, NIV)!"

When we move into this higher realm of relationship with God, we can experience His peace no matter how difficult life becomes. In my dream, there was so much peace in the power of God's presence. This happens when we simply shift our focus from the attacks of the enemy to our love and worship of God!

Father, I recognize the demonic patterns and cycles that have given fear a paralyzing hold on me throughout my life. Forgive me for not living in the freedom that your Son died to give me. I repent and renounce all fear that I have been in participation with: running, hiding, worry, throwing up, stress, anxiety, and panic attacks. Jesus, I choose to lay it all at your feet. I give it all to you now! I refuse all associations, patterns and cycles with every kind of fear: fear of people, fear of failing, fear of places and things that I have given myself to. As an act of my will, I loose all fear from my soul. I break patterns and cycles by the power of the Blood of Jesus. I break every form of fear that keeps me in bondage and turmoil. I choose to lay it all at your feet. The soul tie that has been with me since birth is no longer with me. I renounce all unhealthy soul ties to everything connected with fear. I break mind-controlling spirits and strongholds formed in my mind. I lay down all past traumas at Jesus' feet. And now, I call back every part of my soul and mind that I gave away to fear. I call back my peace, joy, and happiness in the name of Jesus. Amen.

CHAPTER 16

Surrenderering, Are You Quarreling With Your Maker?

I surrendered on my knees. I truly gave Him all that I had at the altar that day, not knowing if it was enough or if He would reject or accept me. Would He love me because of my past, because it was me who walked away from Him? Was it too late? I was crying and so desperate to receive His acceptance. Yet, I felt so unworthy. I had so much inner conflict and turmoil with racing and unbelieving thoughts. I didn't know who I could trust or believe in. I knew God could rescue people, but would He rescue me?

What you believe becomes how you act, which becomes what leads and guides you.

Sometimes we forget or do not realize when God's amazing grace is present on our journey of affliction. We have all sinned, and that's the truth. There is no perfect human on this side of Heaven besides Jesus. Either way, if we are honest with ourselves, we have fallen short of God's glory.

I knew He was more than able, but would He do it for *me*? The power of God is diminished through our doubt and evil foreboding or fearful apprehension. Part of me just wanted to run out of that church. The struggle was intense, but I felt so drawn to be there, needing something more than what the world offered me. The Bible was written to break down unbelief and build up our trust in God. To bring you perfect peace and rest. My pride and my surrender were at odds with one another.

I just knew there had to be more. I desperately wanted the peace, joy, and happiness I saw others have in life. We must all come to that place of surrender with the Lord. He has given us the free will to choose, and His Word urges us to choose Him for ourselves. We have the sovereign power and authority of our will to use in our lives. Your will is the key to your freedom. Choosing is your part. Deliverance is God's part, but we must join our will with His. This is a process we must take to walk in freedom and remove the strongholds we have allowed by being passive. It first starts with you taking responsibility for your life.

The Lord wants your whole heart, but He wants you to give it freely. The Bible tells us *"Even now," declares the LORD, "return to me with all your heart, with fasting and weeping and mourning (Joel 2:12)."* A lack of trust keeps you from a deeper relationship with the Father. The absence of the Father leaves you wondering aimlessly in life, trying to figure it out. We just continue in our brokenness, unbalanced emotions, and chaos.

The hurt and pain of a wounded life hardens the heart, and your will becomes indifferent. It becomes nearly impossible to trust anyone. It is especially hard because we erect walls of self-protection that keep everyone, including the Lord, out. Make a choice to give it all to Him. A severed will (numbness) and hardened heart influence the soul and spirit, so God's Word and spirit cannot penetrate it. Your heart becomes spiritually dead and unresponsive to His calling. When this happens, you become indifferent, then the enemy takes full advantage of your unwillingness to stay engaged. Passivity keeps us from being able to make good choices. We then give other people and the enemy too much control over our lives.

I struggled within, and my wounded heart was full of fearful emotions. I then realized my fears, guilt, and shame were controlling my emotions which became hidden obstacles to my ability to receive and express His love. I didn't even know what love looked like anymore. The enemy kept shouting that I didn't deserve the Father's love. I had not learned that He loves us just as He finds us. He couldn't love us more than when He created us in our mothers' womb. This kind of bad thinking and reckless emotions will control you. It will eventually dam up the river of life. Destructive emotions give the enemy a place to inhib-it the flow of the river of life. It took me years to discover the importance of deliverance and inner healing. It's hard to stop bad thoughts unless you get rid of unpleasant emotions. We can get rid of negative emotions by submitting and choosing to ac-cept God's forgiveness and by choosing to forgive others and ourselves. Walking in freedom starts with making the choice to open your heart to the Lord. You must relinquish all control back to the Lord because your life now belongs to Him. When you do this, you receive His peace, and the inner river of life can flow again. As Jesus said, *"Whoever believes in me, as Scripture has said, rivers of living water will flow from within them (John 7:38, NIV)."*

When we trust God, we choose to receive His healing, and we learn how to get rid of destructive emotions. We receive His love and peace which flows freely just as the river of life flows, bring-ing healing nourishment to our body, and spirit. As our body and spirit heal along with our relationship with the Father, we heal emotionally so that the river of life flows out of us, enabling us to help others.

Believers and unbelievers think they have to get it all right before they can come to God. They think they must be perfect in all their ways, but that is a lie from the enemy. Some lies are generational from foundations built by our ancestors. The lie keeps you from help that only Jesus can give you. Holy help that comes from what Jesus accomplished on the cross. Jesus fin-ished all of our healing on the cross. Our job is to receive that healing by faith.

Many of us have gone a long time without having our emotional needs met, so we have given up all hope of something good. We searched the world and fallen short because we should seek God for all that we need. That is why we are always in a state of longing for more, waiting for more and coming up empty. Are you trying to get your emotional needs met by other people only to be disappointed?

Only God can fill the empty place in your heart. The feelings of dissatisfaction keep us yearning after the Father. Our surrender is the breakthrough we so desperately need. It's where the desires of our hearts are. Our emotional healing only comes from Him. Emotional voids are filled when we spend intimate time with God through worship, prayer, and the Word of God. I'm done chasing people for my happiness, only to be let down. I have tried to do it on my own, in my own way, and in my strength, only to discover I need Him more than anything else. He is your first love, the One who calls you, and the only One who truly knows you.

I'm here to tell you that God is proud of your chosen salvation and if you are not, the Holy Spirit is drawing you to Him. Jesus died to cover every sin for every person. *Isaiah 1:18, NIV says, "Come now, let us settle the matter," says the LORD. "Though your sins are like scarlet, they shall be as white as snow; though they are red as crimson, they shall be like wool."* He is patient with you, not wanting anyone to perish, but everyone to come to repentance (See *Psalms 51:6-10*). Emotional healing will release the past blockages and patterns and allow profound spiritual growth to take place. You will grow in the knowledge and understanding of your spiritual gift.

We must confess and repent for our sins at the altar. We must humbly come before the Lord. Bow your knee in remembrance of Jesus, the one true living sacrifice for all of humankind. Christ in us, the hope of glory! The old man passes away and the new man comes forth, *"... we are transformed, washed clean, set free as willing vessels for his great use (1 Corinthians 6:11)."*

Through your repentance, little by little, He brings you through to healing and freedom from all that has made you a prisoner of war. Jesus works through your surrendered state. Emotional healing allows us to come to terms with events and circumstances which have occurred in our lives and let them go. Once the emotional healing work has released past emotional bondages and blockages, we can integrate these experiences into our lives, allowing ourselves to grow and develop emotionally on a deeper, more profound spiritual level. Your greatest inheritance is that which you overcome for yourself and your future generations.

As we overcome through healing, God levels out the controlling highs and lows of our emotions. Our emotions are no longer a runaway rollercoaster. Carrying emotional blockages prevents us from moving forward in our spiritual journey. Emotional healing will release past blockages and patterns and allow profound spiritual growth to take place. An overwhelmingly negative event that causes a lasting impact on our mental and emotional stability can cause trauma. While many sources of trauma exist, they can leave a lasting negative impression in our hearts.

I came to the Lord with a hardened heart and severed will. He greeted me with open arms. He was just waiting for me to surrender at His feet. Trying to figure it all out exhausted me. He already knows how we have sinned against Him, but He will wash us clean through the Word of God. This means that God is willing to set us free from all of our transgressions when we decide to repent because of His love for us. "Salvation is a supernatural work of God. Come as you are, but you won't stay as you are because God is working in true believers. God doesn't want something from us. He simply wants us." -C.S. Lewis[30]

Jesus is the heart surgeon, but we can only surrender to the capacity that our heart allows. We must be willing and obedient to do what God asks. Our lack of trust, lack of cooperation, and disobedience blocks Him from working and keeps us stuck.

Consider how precious a soul must be when both God and the devil are after it." -CH Spurgeon[31]

Whether or not you realize it, you are either being pulled to the altar of God or the enemy is pulling you to his altar of destruction. I must ask you whose altar are you kneeling at? There really is no gray area. Pride, rebellion, and stubbornness are the

30. Chery, F., 2022. 22 Important Bible Verses About Come As You Are. [online] Bible Reasons | Bible Verses About Various Topics. Available at: <https://biblereasons.com/come-as-you-are/> [Accessed 20 March 2022].

31. https://www.cslewis.org/blog/a-word-of-grace-march-14-2011/

work of witchcraft. Is it possible you could unknowingly operate out of the wrong spirit? It shocked me to know that I was and had no idea.

If there is a curse of witchcraft in your bloodline, a familiar spirit will draw you to the dark side little by little. A spirit of witchcraft will have you seeking out prophets for a word. You will become caught up seeking man or witches for a word of your future instead of God. If there is no relationship with the one true God, the enemy will bring temptation to get you at his altar. Here are some examples of witchcraft:

- Rebellion and stubbornness
- the Ouija board
- magic 8 ball
- horoscopes
- palm readers
- psychics
- mediums
- acupuncture
- new age
- yoga
- scary movies
- gossip and slander.

What do slander, gossip, and New Age philosophy, have to do with witchcraft? I hope you will understand their spiritual connection as we explore the answer together. We know slander is false charges against someone. The Ninth Commandment says, "You shall not give false testimony."

What does the Bible say about gossip? (*1 Timothy 5:13 ESV*), is very clear, when it says, "Besides that, they learn to be idlers, going about from house to house, and not only idlers, but also gossips and busybodies, saying what they should not."

New Age beliefs do have an influence on people because they learn two things:

1. Their own experiences are the primary source of authority on spiritual matters.

2. There is no one true way to pursue spirituality.

In (*John 15:1*), Jesus says, "I am the true vine, and in (*John 14:6*), Jesus says, "I am the way, the truth, and the life. No one comes to the Father except through Me."

As we saw with Scripture, slander, gossip, and New Age beliefs are contrary to God's Word, and should be avoided. Listen closely to what I'm about to say: when a person knows what not to do, and continues to do it without repenting quickly, it is sin, rebellion, and pride, which are all included in witchcraft. The concept of witchcraft is a presumption you can continue to do things God has told you not to do without His judgment. That's why repentance, or turning away from sin, is so important. (*Matthew 3:2*) reminds us, "Repent, for the kingdom of heaven is at hand."

If you choose to come into agreement with any of these things, you can bring yourself and your future generations under a curse. Therefore, the condition of your heart and soul is very important because it affects every relationship you have, most importantly your relationship with your Father in Heaven. Jesus told us to pray, *"Our Father who art in heaven... (Luke 11:2-4 KJV)."* We should come as children seated in heavenly places to approach His throne of grace. I think of times when I have experienced the greatest anointing and breakthroughs in my life. These times were always when I was surrendered and worshipped God with all my heart — soaking up His presence, while speaking or reading His Word aloud as a prayer to God the Father.

There is nothing better than the love of the Father. His presence is a treasure. His love is a firm foundation on which you can stand. There is joy and life that never ends. The Holy Spirit, within us, conflicts with our fleshly desires, urging us into relationship and service to Him. Put your focus on things above so you can hear the heartbeat of God. Grab onto the eternal things of God.

We must long to stay in His presence. It's where we belong! We were born for love and worship of God. When we experience God's love, we are more able to bless people by sharing the Father's love, and it increases our love for others. It creates in us a greater capacity to love and serve others because our needs are being met.

In those times, nothing else matters. We should strengthen ourselves at the altar. During a time of prayer, I could hear the Lord calling me to a greater surrender. I honestly thought I had given the Lord my whole heart, but something was blocking me. I cried out to Him, asking Him what the block was or what felt like a dam clogged up from allowing the Holy Spirit to flow through me like a river. I knew that something was wrong, that there was a root somewhere that I was unaware of. I had pushed down years of emotional trauma and feelings. God took me deeper into a greater surrender through the revelation of His love for me.

Sometimes it would trickle and other times there would be nothing. I kept hearing someone calling my name and there wouldn't be anyone there in the natural. I later learned that it was the Lord calling me higher so He could balance out the highs and lows. Letting go is in your surrender. It is in your laying it all down. We must trust in God in order to let go. Release it all back to God and forgive who needs to be forgiven. The happiest times in my life have been when I've let go of all that I couldn't change or control that bogged me down. Letting go preceeds what is coming in your future. Your past or past circumstances should not hold you back. Put your trust in God and let your faith supersede the past while choosing to let go. Consider what God has planned for your future. Stop looking back. You are not going that way. You must release the past to focus on the future.

It takes courage to move into the unknown. It's time to take inventory and embrace where you need healing. What do you need to let go of? Before a new thing can come forth, you must let go of the past. We all have pride, regrets, failures, heartache, and loss of dreams that need to be laid at the altar, but sorrow and grief lead us inward. Often, we retreat inward, isolating ourselves from the people we love and everyday life. How often do we just give up because we fear the past and don't really understand what He is asking us to do with it? The broken-hearted unknowingly and desperately hold on to all of their pain, burdens, and grief instead of releasing it to Him at the altar. Broken people have a very hard time letting go of the past, which hinders their moving into the future. God uses your encounter at the altar to bring dead things back to life. This is where the fire of God brings dead hearts back to life. There is fire on the altar to transform. It is a place where you can release your pain and burdens. Come to Him and receive forgiveness, healing, and freedom.

He must purge out all of what has happened to you. When you have years of built-up anguish suppressed and bottled up deep inside of your heart like I did, it creates a barrier between your spirit and the Spirit of God, which stops the flow of the river of life that flows from the throne of grace. Therefore, we cannot refuse to go back to that place because it's a painful place. God reveals it in order to heal us. Sometimes you must be uncomfortable to become comfortable. The Lord kept asking me to go back to that place in the past and let Him in so he could heal my heart in an instant.

I didn't want to go back and relive the traumas, so I kept refusing to go there, even though it was my heart's cry to be free. I couldn't see it. My natural mind couldn't comprehend what my spirit was trying to convey because I didn't have enough knowledge of God to understand what had a hold of me. I didn't understand the forces of evil working against my life and my generations. I knew something was wrong, but I couldn't, for the life of me, figure out what it was or how to change it. I just kept getting caught up in the repetitive cycles. It honestly took years of searching and intercessory prayer.

Does your heart hunger and thirst for breakthrough, for something deeper? That yearning is your Savior. He is the sacrificial lamb drawing you closer to Himself. The altar is where all humankind can move toward redemption. Everything changes at the altar. God knows our desires and wants to know us in a more intimate and powerful way. His altar is always open. The Holy Spirit is drawing us there. The altar is the place of surrender.

The Lord is calling us all to a place of intercession and surrender. It's more than just prayer. Its confession and consecration as we devote it all to Christ. The altar doesn't have to be at church. It is wherever you want to give it all to God. It can be at home, a prayer meeting, or a worship gathering. He will meet you in your surrender right where you are at. The altar is about our trust, humility, surrender and sacrifice to God. Without it, it is impossible to have a genuine relationship with the Father. The Lord requires righteousness, consecration, and holiness from us. He desires you to give Him your whole heart before you bring Him your needs. So many are broken and beaten up by the enemy that they do not trust the Lord enough to surrender it all to Him.

He knows exactly what we need. The altar is a place of hope, restoration, and victory. The altar is where your joy, peace, strength, and hope are renewed. We receive healing in our soul and spirit. A surrendered and healed heart becomes a heart on fire, which becomes a radical vessel for the Kingdom. We must pass on to our future generations how to have a relationship with God at the altar, so they do not fall prey to the schemes of the enemy and end up at the wrong altar. Some people will kneel at the altar of Satan on purpose, and there are people who Satan draws in unsuspectingly. Once he has a hold on you from the hatred in your heart, that hatred and anger develop into rebellion. Rebellion fights in your flesh against all that is godly in your spirit. I remember that intense battle between my flesh and spirit once I received Christ.

I would feel my spirit trying to draw me closer to the Lord, but I had a resistance deep within me that refused to be led. I would hear the Lord asking me to get on my knees before Him and I desperately wanted to, but I just couldn't find it in myself to obey Him. When you have lived most of your life in chaos and turmoil, there is a deep root of resistance and rebellion that has to be overcome. The lack of trust would not allow me to trust Him enough to let Him in.

The Jezebel spirit passed down from generation to generation, operates in rebellion until someone stands up to it and renounces it, breaking the spell over your mind. Disobedience and rebellion will cause you to lose focus of everything around you and the light becomes dim. God will allow you to remain in the same place until you surrender to His will and plan. Pride will cause you to rebel against all truth that which is godly.

James 4:7-8 TPT, "So then, surrender to God. Stand up to the devil and resist him and he will turn and run away from you. Move your heart closer and closer to God and he will come even closer to you but make sure you cleanse your life, you sinners and keep your heart pure and stop doubting."

I heard Him say, "Come to the altar." I said, "Lord, what does that mean?" I would ask pastors and other Christians what that meant to them. Unfortunately, they didn't know either. As I sought this out, I went to a church meeting, and the preacher spoke about...You guessed it, the Altar. He said, "Come into the inner courts of the tabernacle, the secret place, where we can meet with the Father."

I really wanted to meet with Him, but I just couldn't bring myself to do what He wanted me to do. He wanted my whole heart. He wanted the good, the bad and the ugly so that He could make me whole. You don't have to be ashamed anymore, you just have to come. The blood of Jesus is enough to take you into the Holy of Holies. The blood of the Lamb takes us into the secret place. One genuine encounter with the Living God will change your life forever. A love encounter, where Heaven meets the earth, will touch your heart forever. You will come to the sudden realization of His love for you. In His presence, you will find the love He has for you and all the afflictions will fade away. In the presence of the Lord, there is such peace in knowing that we need Him, and we are finally home.

Our love for Him grows as our perception of Him changes in those transformational instances of His illuminating love.

We realize that we were born to commune with our Creator, the Father. After years of crying out to God for help, I realized it was me who was refusing what was right in front of me. He loves us way too much to just leave us where we are. I would like to share this testimony with you, so you can have a real-life experience to help you understand what I mean. The experience completely wrecked me, but it was exactly what I needed.

I went to receive prayer with a group of ladies that were experienced in emotional healing. I had never met these ladies before in my life, which I'm thankful for because I could just let it all out without having to withhold anything for fear of judgement. I have been involved in deliverance ministry, so I thought I knew what to expect. Boy was I wrong. I never expected what happened.

We started out by worshipping God and praising His glorious name. They told me to ask God who I needed to forgive. I had my idea on the way there of who that was, and even though I had some forgiving to do for them, they were not the intended target. I began to sing and ask God who it was, and He quickly reminded me of a situation with my husband from the night before. I told the ladies that the night before there was a heated verbal disagreement with my husband and I needed to forgive Him.

They had agreed that my husband was definitely the reason I was there. They told me to think of 4-5 things I needed to forgive him for. After 30 years of marriage, it isn't hard to do. So, I gave them my reasons. The next part really wrecked me. She said, "Now we want you to tell your husband exactly how he made you feel in each of these instances." I was like a deer in headlights because I realized in that moment, I had not expressed to him how I felt for years because it didn't seem to matter anymore how I felt.

It was a sad and painful realization. I choked out the words, one situation at a time, crying all the more as I went from the least to the most painful experience. I was crying so hard as the old emotions and feelings surfaced. A part of me just wanted to get up and run out the door. I knew that if I left, I would never get past this place emotionally. Thankfully, I was in a very safe place with godly women who were filled with compassion and love for Christ.

As I expressed the pain from years of negative verbal assaults and treatment, the tears would not stop falling. I was so overwhelmed by what I was experiencing I couldn't contain it. A fresh wind of His Spirit washed over me. I was able to forgive him for layers upon layers that were keeping me dammed up. I had just been shoving the hurts down.

I had shoved them for so long that I had lost who I was. Because I allowed someone to squash the life right out of me, my heart was broken. I was neglecting my own heart's cry as I was inwardly silenced. I was just going through the motions, just trying to survive. The Lord spoke to me during this time and said, "Alena, I need you to do more than survive. I need you to thrive and move into what I have called you to do."

I left there crying continually. A floodgate had opened, and it just kept coming and coming. The next day I woke up mad. I felt like God had taken me back to the place of where I started shutting down. I couldn't figure out why or what I was supposed to do with the fear, anger, and self-hatred that came up. I was so mad at myself for the way I felt and for just letting it build up to that point.

I began to pray in the Spirit. As I did, I had so much anguish. I started yelling at God, "I DON'T KNOW WHAT YOU WANT FROM ME." I just kept crying and yelling it over and over. There were years I wanted to leave, and the Lord said no. I couldn't imagine why He wanted me to stay until now, writing this book. It is all making sense now. I realized I was so mad at God for all that I endured by staying.

Everything I had endured in my life seemed so unfair. I was in a rage that was illuminating from my body. When I followed Christ, I did not know that I would walk through so much all alone, with little or no help. The path was so narrow. I couldn't step to the right or left without some kind of reprimand from God. I would hear people talk about the love of God, His mercy and grace, but I felt like He was more of a disciplinarian on my journey.

I had the help of the Holy Spirit, but I didn't know what a treasure that was until I began to see things through God's eyes. I felt like I was being trained harder than most people I knew that were walking with Jesus. The training was intense. The opposition, trials, and transitions were so challenging for some-one who didn't understand what was going on. After I realized how mad at God I was, I could repent and release it all from my soul.

God is uprooting all that is in you that is in opposition to the truth of His Word. The revelation of His truth that is coming forth out of the deepest places in your heart and soul. He is sepa-rating you from the fleshly, carnal things of this world. It takes great faith to walk in His power and strength.

I couldn't continue to be held back by the things of the past. I had to let go to grow deeper in the things of God. The unfor-giveness of the past was holding me hostage and keeping me from the abundant life God's Word promises us. My husband and I were both in a place of brokenness. We were just two peo-ple trying to save each other, blindly trying to find our way, and barely surviving because of all that we had both endured.

Neither of us wanted to surrender to each other, much less to God. Hurting people hurt people. I wouldn't be telling the truth if I didn't admit that I wasn't always nice to him, either. I know that I have caused him some heartache and emotional trauma, as well. We have both had to apologize and forgive each other in order for our marriage to be healed and restored.

When there is a lack of honor and respect in your life, you will always be in a position of self-protecting, which creates loneli-ness and rejection. I didn't respect anyone because of the lack of respect and the betrayals I had experienced. I became very rebellious in trying to defend myself. I didn't know that God was my defender, and that he would vindicate me in my humility and submission. When your heart becomes numb, you lose all godly perception of honor and respect.

It mortified me to learn that if you won't submit to those in authority, you will not submit to God. I remember desperately wanting everything in my life to change, especially in my marriage to my husband, Kevin. I had already exhausted every effort that I knew. I read books on marriage, I prayed, fasted with little change. It was so frustrating, and I wanted to just quit and give up. I wanted to walk away. Actually, I wanted to run away as fast as I could, but the Lord wanted me to stay. I knew that if I left, I would be out of the will of the Lord.

I didn't understand why until years later. Running seemed much easier because I had no other solution. Sometimes when things in our lives don't change, it's because the Lord is trying to change something in own heart. He uses uncomfortable circumstances in our lives to expose what is in our hearts so He can heal us. When you run during the difficult times in life, nothing in your life gets resolved or healed.

You just become a wandering soul, going from place to place, or from relationship to relationship because nothing is being dealt with. You take it all with you everywhere. It is just easier to blame everyone else for the condition of our own lives because then we don't have to focus on ourselves. I would cry out to God, wanting Him to fix my husband because I sincerely thought that he was the problem. I couldn't see the plank in my eye. He thought I was the problem, so we were in a battle, a tug of war, and both of us wanted to be right. I remember the Lord asking me one day, "Do you want to be right, or do you want to have peace?"

I honestly had to ponder on that for a while because my flesh wanted to be right and my spirit wanted peace, exposing more of that internal war. My flesh wanted to be in control because it had become very accustomed to that position, but it was clearly ruling over my spirit, which was causing an alignment issue with God. Every time I would cry out about an injustice, the Lord would remind me, "I'm not talking to you about him. I'm talking to you about what is in your heart."

I had become such a victim that I couldn't see my own faults of my bitter and vengeful heart. There are two spirits in operation: the spirit of the devil and the spirit of God. When we allow our flesh to rule and reign, the enemy has the upper hand in our lives. When we surrender and submit to the work of the Holy Spirit, the spirit of God is in control of our lives. The Bible tells us in 1 *Chronicles 16:27 KJV, "Glory and honor are in His presence; strength and gladness are in His place."* When we do His will, do His good works, it is by His mercy and grace. Paul tells us, *"For we are his workmanship, having been created in Christ Jesus for good works that God prepared beforehand so we may do them (Ephesians 2:10, NET)."*

It is by His prompting that we are being drawn deeper. It's in the secret place with Him where healing begins. It's in that deeper place we gain knowledge and wisdom of the ways of God.

I was completely unaware of the daily sin I was living in by not being in submission to my husband and to God. I heard the Lord say, "Alena, If you do not submit to your husband, you will never fully surrender to me." I just could not, for the life of me, figure out how the two went together. I had been hurt way too much to trust my husband, and submission wasn't an option. To be perfectly honest, my pride just didn't want to do it. I would try to rationalize my behavior and inability to give up my position because of fear. My fear and pride were controlling all of my decisions and it was destroying my relationships with the people I loved the most — most importantly, God. I was blind to the error of my ways. I would ask God, why do you want me to follow someone who doesn't know where He is going? I mean, he isn't attending church or serving you. It did not logically make any sense for me to submit and follow him. It went against everything I was taught growing up.

Upon submitting, I later learned that it had nothing to do with where my husband was spiritually. It had everything to do with my pride and rebellion. I was striving because of the perception of how I thought it would be. I was creating a safe place of self-protection for me to never surrender and love with all of my heart so I would not get hurt again.

When our identity is not grounded in Christ, we end up juggling unbalanced emotions, and temptation rushes in to make us doubt our holiness. You must resist that lie because you are holy in Christ Jesus, and you must believe with all your heart and trust in the Holy Spirit's protection. Your actions and choices represent you. Your mindset must change and line up with the

Word of God. From salvation there was an exchange, and you became God's undeniably the minute you accepted His gift of redemption. He paid the price for your sins! He said, "It is finished on the cross!"

If you want your glory to increase, your flesh must die daily. This is a painful process, but there is no other way. Do you ever wonder why it appears the enemy has the upper hand? Why are so many living defeated lives? I believe they do not know who God is and they do not know their identity or authority in Christ. They're too afraid to bring it all to the altar. We must stop tolerating the enemy. Stop allowing him to distract you from your time with the Lord at the altar. God has given us authority over the enemy, but so few are using this authority, they remain stuck in a cycle of consistent attack.

We are in a war between our flesh and spirit. In order for our spirit to rise higher to its rightful place, we must humble ourselves before God and allow Him to cut the cords that entangle us. We have some powerful weapons in our arsenal as children of God that we must engage in the battle. So, take your position of humility and hold firm the weapons in your arsenal. Recognize, admit, and confess your sin and shortcomings to God. Be truthful about where you are and do not blame others. Be quick to repent. Worship even when you don't feel like it. Plead the blood of Jesus, declare power in the name of Jesus. Declare the Word of God. Make your praise and thanksgiving known to Him. Receive the power of the Holy Spirit. Be quick in your obedience, praying for your enemies, those who persecute you and those who betray you. Here is a list of some obstacles that will distract you from the altar: sin, guilt, shame, condemnation, embarrassment from not being able to have victory, chaos, mind battles, wasting time, fighting the wrong war, dead works, fear, doubt, and lack of trust. These obstacles can steal your time with the Lord at the altar.

PRAYER FOR A CLEANSED HEART

Let us now take a moment to consider all we have discussed. Let's begin to take advantage of this time with God. Pray this prayer: "God, I ask you in this moment to give me the strength to let go of every ancient and worldly structure, all disobedience, rebellion, pride, false identity, reputation, previous success or failures that I have held onto dearly. Give me the grace to come to a place of absolute surrender of my old life. Help me lay it all on the altar. I ask for your fire to come and burn all that is not of you. As I surrender everything I've known and lay my life at your feet, I also invite the Holy Spirit to come and fill every cell in my body with your power. Give me the courage I will need to welcome the new that you have for me in this season, regardless of what it looks or feels like. I want more of you, Jesus, no matter what the cost. Let my heart explode with love for you and your people. Help me recognize my need for you today. Father, give me a greater revelation and knowledge of your love for me so that I may know my true identity and purpose on the earth. God create in me a new heart for this season. Give me a new wineskin for the new wine that you are pouring out. Give me a new mind to know you more. Fill my life with new hopes, dreams, visions, and a new reality of your amazing love. Give me a new capacity to connect more deeply with you than ever before. Lord, birth a new thing in and through me for such a time as this. Yes and Amen, and let it be so for your glory, King Jesus!"

PROCLAMATIONS FOR A CLEAN START
Based on Ephesians 5:1-5

I will imitate God and follow His example. I will walk in love as Christ loved me and gave Himself up for me, a slain offering, sacrificed to God, a sweet fragrance. I will have good morals, pure and generous, as is fitting for God's consecrated people. I will allow no filthy or foolish, sinful, or coarse jesting to come out of my mouth. I have an inheritance in the Kingdom of God. I am a child of light. I constantly produce good fruit - kindness, goodness, uprightness of heart and trueness of life. I am learning to please God and live a life that is acceptable to Him. Amen.

CHAPTER 17

Release Control

Are you looking for some relief? Are you frustrated because your circumstances are not changing? I felt oppressed, depressed, and frustrated because circumstances caught me in the same cycles, the same patterns in life, like a hamster on a wheel. I walked in my flesh and soulish [mind, will, emotions] area instead of being led by the Holy Spirit. This leads to dead works and performance/perfectionism.

I had to release control of my life to the Father. This took some time because I was broken, rebellious, stubborn, and prideful. I did not understand God or His ways. You see, His ways are not our ways or the ways of the world. To grow from Glory to Glory, we must conform to God's image.

God's greatest character trait is His love. If we cannot receive His love, then we truly have nothing to give away to others.

The enemy is relentless in making people feel like God is mad at them and that He does not love them.

This is one of the biggest lies I believed. I could not see or feel His love. I was unaware of the ways of God and what He was trying to do through my life. I was trying to understand the pain in the process of what I was enduring because I had experienced a very unstable childhood, which left me overcome with despair, disappointment, and discouragement. From an incredibly young age, I battled generational curses and the powers of darkness.

The battles you are engaged in are from the enemy, who comes to steal everything he can before you are even aware there is an enemy.

The enemy sets out to destroy you as early as he can. Often, it is in the womb. He plots our destruction most often from birth, especially when God has planned greatness for your life. It is the image of God within us that provokes him to hate us.

Unbeknownst to us, we follow the enemies' lies and deceptions because we have no clue of the war that rages in and around us. This leaves us feeling like a victim. This is when we allow our spiritual selves to become disconnected from our life source. This is when a person's heart becomes spiritually dead, indifferent, hopeless, and despairing in life, because it is the spirit of God that sustains and upholds us. The enemy lies about who God is, His faithfulness, His goodness, and His love for all humankind.

Our pain affects our perspective of how we view others, and how others view us! When we filter through our past hurts, rejections, and experiences, we find it impossible to believe what God's Word says about us or Him. It directly affects our relationship with the Father, our view and reception of His word, faithfulness, goodness, and love. To know God is to know love.

It took time and healing for me to realize that I was on a journey with the Lord and He was doing a mighty work in my life. He wanted me healed from the past. The Holy Spirit was my lifeline to the Father. The Holy Spirit spoke to me. I learned to hear and obey the Holy Spirit, instead of my fleshly and worldly ways.

In order to follow the leading of the Holy Spirit, I had to relinquish my desires and way of life up to this point. True obedience unto the Lord must be a lifestyle. You must allow the Holy Spirit to lead and guide you. Your obedience will move the heart of God!

God will use everything in our past, no matter how painful it is. He considers it experience. Many of us have gone through difficult things and those things qualify us to help someone else on their journey, so let go of old mindsets, ways, and patterns. Broken vessels know exactly what others are experiencing because they have been in the trenches. Through our experience, we gain firsthand knowledge of how we made it through.

Please remember that kids raised in chaos become adults in chaos who repeat the cycle until someone works diligently with the Holy Spirit to break the demonic structures and cycles.

CHAPTER 18

Final Glory

Dear broken and shattered one, have you ever wondered why there are so many who are not living the life that Christ died to give them? I have thought of this many times over the years and asked God, "Why this is so prevalent? Why are your people living a life of bondage, crushed in spirit and in slavery to the enemy instead of the complete victory that we read about in the Word of God? Why is our natural living not lining up with the Word of God? What are we missing?"

I truly believe that a lack of knowledge and understanding is the main reason why many are not living according to the sacrifice of Christ. People are perishing for a lack of knowledge of who God is, His character and His endless love for people are unaware of their identities which are made in His image through Christ. Doubt and unbelief outweigh the truth in the lives of so many who have had their innocence stolen by the enemy. The following is a dream I had about how doubt affects the lives of wounded believers.

I found myself in a cathedral. I walked in on a lower level, looking all around. I was amazed at how breathtaking and beautiful it was. I then found myself at the highest level. Not even thinking about what I was doing, I walked right out into the air, admiring how magnificent it was. I looked down and started to panic and doubt. Why did I walk out here? What was I thinking? I'm going to fall. As soon as I began to doubt and agree in my thoughts, I began to decline and move downward. About halfway down, the Holy Spirit rose up from within me and I began to declare with a loud shout, "THERE IS POWER IN THE BLOOD. THERE IS POWER IN THE NAME OF JESUS. THERE IS POWER IN THE WORD OF GOD."

As I was declaring this out loud, I began to ascend upward. I rose up to the highest place with ease. I learned from this dream that when I would doubt and fear, I would go down low. When I would have faith in the power of Jesus, the Blood of Jesus, and the Word of God, I would ascend upon high to the Holy place. I could be in the secret place with the Lord. Don't allow doubt and unbelief to keep you in a low place. Allow your faith and power weapons to keep you in the throne room high above where the enemy can go.

Psalms 34:17-18 (AMPC), "When the righteous cry out for help, the Lord hears, delivers them out of all their distress and troubles. The Lord is close to those who are of a broken heart and saves such as are crushed with sorrow from sin and are humbly and thoroughly penitent."

The Father will go to great lengths to rescue and restore your broken heart and crushed spirit. Be confident and courageous that God is with you and on your side. You are not forgotten or alone. There is no distance too far away for God to find you. Regardless of how much despair, sorrow, grief, sadness, depression, or fear have gripped your mind, soul, and spirit; your circumstances will push you to destiny. Allow God to wake you up to His reality. Self-pity is the glue that keeps you stuck there. Once a stronghold is established, it is often not easy to escape from. It takes great diligence to overcome. Every person has some kind of darkness in their mind to overcome.

You can have wealth, education, success, and satisfaction and still be poor in spirit. You cannot get from a man what only Jesus can do in your heart and soul. Jesus said that man could not take His place. We often look for people to heal our broken hearts, but Jesus is our redeemer and healer. The Blood of Jesus washes away the broken-hearted, the broken will, and spirit. The pain in your heart has to be dealt with. If not, it just layers of hurt over the other. Ask the Lord to heal your heart and purge out all the years your heart has been neglected.

He uses the emotional and physical things in this life to deplete and drain you of all hope. You lose sight of your dreams. He will get you so distracted and on the run in your mind that you can't think straight. You become paralyzed and fixated on what the enemy is doing instead of how glorious God is and what He is capable of doing. It is terrible to be crushed in spirit, but it is in the crushing that God shines a spotlight on all that hinders our relationship with Him. God brings forth valuable hidden beauty when we experience being crushed and betrayed in our hearts and emotions. Our tragedy and misfortune can bring forth Kingdom fruit if we get to the altar and give Him access. Allow Him to work it all out His way. He will bring forth the revelation and knowledge that we need as we seek Him.

When roses are crushed, the fragrance comes forth. When olives are crushed, they bring forth oil, and when grapes are crushed, they bring forth wine. He knows what you need before you even ask. He hears your cries of despair and sees every tear you've cried. He knows exactly where to find you. He reveals the hidden areas of your heart so they can be healed.

He uses winter storms to bring forth the new growth in spring. He uses all things in our hearts that need attention. You are learning to pray and use your authority in every trial or test. Don't retreat. Stand and fight. The enemy will try to shut you up and shut you down! Do not allow the enemy to steal from you because you tolerate him.

"Storms come to the good and the bad, the holy and the unholy. Quit waving the surrender flag. Take your position. Earthly comfort will never lead to breakthrough. God will lead us in the fire, the storm, the unknown and the unseen. The Word of God will outlast every storm. Storms eventually run out of rain. Jesus is the master of every storm. The sun will shine again. Storms can redirect you to the place God wants you to be." – Dr. James Payne

In the story of Moses, the Israelites cried out to God to be delivered and set free. God called Moses to be their deliverer and set them free from the bondages that beset them. It didn't take long for Moses to realize that he could not help them because they would not allow him to lead them out of the place they were in the past. Their captive mindset kept pulling them back to what was familiar, even though they were miserable. I believe many have decided the journey is too hard, and they have returned to their Egypt. I completely understand. I felt like that many times along the way, but our mindset has to be fixed on the Lord, so we are never tempted to give up and return to bondage.

Many decided the journey was too hard and returned to Egypt to submit to what is familiar. They have chosen to remain in bondage and slavery because it is easier than facing the obstacles of an unknown road. Doubt and unbelief reflect the contradictions in our souls, fears, and wounds in our hearts. The spirit of faith addresses the cast down soul and puts the focus back on God. The enemy uses distractions and thoughts of doubt to flood your mind because he knows doubt steals your faith. He knows the chaos he creates can get you fighting the wrong fight.

Satan will lead you in to dead works, and doing it all in your own strength. We must make a conscious effort to choose faith and relinquish all control to God. Your emotions and feelings will lead you astray. You must choose your actions based on the Word of God. The Bible is written to break down unbelief and build up your trust and faith in God to bring you to perfect peace and rest in Him. No matter how narrow the road has been, or how broken your heart has become from crying out from the pit of despair, you must choose life which is the power of your testimony.

To tell your story is to tell of Christ. Your life is a message needed by God to further advance the Kingdom. You are a threat to the enemy. He hates you because you are a child of God. God loves you way too much to leave you in this condition. He sent Jesus to rescue and deliver you.

Jesus paid the ultimate price so you could live with God under His protection. Our old life died with the resurrection. It should have been left behind with the grave. God didn't give you a new life in Christ only to have you continue in a sinful nature or to remain operating in your old ways.

God only sees the new you in Christ. He absolutely loves you! Your newness of life is your gift with the Holy Spirit reconciled to the Father. You must learn to partner with the Holy Spirit in order to become one with Him. This is where we come to the end of self and are awakened to the transforming power of the cross. Every believer has a voice, and it is a voice of victory (Graham Cooke).

A change in the heart changes the attitude. He reveals to heal. Prayer is working and communing with God with unbroken, uninterrupted fellowship to fulfill His perfect will and resolve our hearts' issues. Our spirit is our power source that connects us to

God. The enemy works hard to crush our spirit, push us down, and hold us there to muzzle our prophetic voices.

When you are weary and frustrated, you have taken your eyes off Him. You have lost your way. Our souls are anchored to the ways of the world, worldly people, and the familiarity of the past. When we fix our eyes on His love, He makes us whole for the world to see.

A changed life is the reflection of Jesus glorified.

When you are in the toughest battles, you can be tempted to want God to take it all away. If you stop now, where would your relationship with God be? Would you be satisfied just staying where you are and not moving forward? When we walk it out and walk through it, we develop a deeper relationship with the Lord. We learn so much if we pay attention. We learn to pray and war. We learn that He is faithful and good. Our faith is made stronger, and our trust is without borders.

You may feel like you have been trained harder than anyone else. The Lord has worked through you in steps of faith and now He will work through you with leaps of faith. Your foundation has been established. Allow the Holy Spirit to heal the cracks in your foundation so that you can carry the heavy load of the Kabod Glory.

The Kabod, as mentioned in the Old Testament 34 times, means "The glory of the Lord." Or "Praise be to the Lord" It's a way of witnessing His radiant beauty. It has also been mentioned as being related to something heavy, both physically and figuratively. Take, for example, *Exodus 17:12* (Moses' hands were heavy.) So, in essence, the word means something weighty and heavy that glorifies the Lord.[32]

Your present trials are meant to wake you up to the manifested glory of God that is to be revealed in you! You are created in the image of God Almighty and are a divine display of His purpose on the earth. Give yourself room to not be perfect, knowing you aren't Jesus Christ. The enemy tries to fight you on this point of perfection because the love of God in Christ Jesus is perfecting us.

God isn't looking for perfect vessels, but willing and surrendered ones. He already knows our imperfections but He loves us anyway. He already accepted you. Jesus called Peter to come to him and without thought, Peter walked on the water. Jesus called to him, "Come as you are!" He is waiting on you! Daily drawing you into His kingdom just the way you are, knowing fully that it is the love of God that is in Christ Jesus. He is perfecting you. You should allow God Almighty to perfect His love in you so that He can bring you into the fullness of that love. You must learn to live in a place of acceptance in the beloved.

---

32. Celine. "Difference between Kavod and Shekina." Difference Between Similar Terms and Objects, August 15, 2013. http://www.differencebetween.net/miscellaneous/culture-miscellaneous/difference-between-kavod-and-shekina/.

Jesus is calling out to the broken and hurting who are overwhelmed by the weight of their sin. He is prompting you to hear His voice singing over you. The Holy Spirit is blowing in the rhythm of the wind, hovering over you, encircling all around and about you, calling out to you so that you won't go under. Come to the defender of your heart. There is a special grace when the heart is under fire. When I was down in the valley, the King of love came down and grabbed me up. He opened up the heavens and pulled me up. I remember the time He pulled me out and called my name.

I brought my broken pieces to the One who saves, and He put the pieces back together, one at a time. The Lord made me whole again. There is no time to wait. Jesus is calling you to come to the secret place with Him, where stone hearts are broken up by the power of His hand. He is breaking new ground so bow down before Him until He is Lord over all. You must leave all your regrets and sorrows behind to make room for the new life that's springing forth. Take off those grave clothes. There isn't anyone in the grave any longer. You're trading beauty for ashes, praise for heaviness, and joy for your mourning.

We are forever changed into the image of His love. He has always been an all-consuming fire. That refining fire brings forth the dross. The Lord meets you with fire on the altar. My life has been forged and tried by holy fire. This is my life, Lord. Consumed in fire that burns away everything that's not of you. Let your glory come and revive hearts to life. The Spirit of the living God lives on the inside of you, changing you from glory to glory.

Jesus named Himself the resurrection and the life. He conquered the grave and came out of it with a resurrection anointing. The devil cannot kill what God is doing in you or through you on the Earth. He cannot stop the move of God. Jesus went into the grave as the Son of man, but came out of the grave as the Son of God. We are coming up out of the grave by the power of the resurrection of God.

What was killed in the grave is not what is coming out of the grave. Jesus transformed the world by the glory and the power of God. God raised the dead. This promise is fulfilled by God whenever human ability doesn't line up with His supernatural ability. Glory comes when man cannot do it. When there is absolutely no possibility that a man can do it, God comes in glory and power.

Before a resurrection, there will be a betrayal to take your hope away. Jesus was betrayed by a friend. The pattern is the same. Though death occurs, it is going to be defeated. Just believe. Walk in the supernatural, in His likeness. God is looking for believers with great faith. Eternal life reigns over death. Death can not and will not stand.

Jesus is life! He rose from the grave to empty out the graveyard. He commanded death to go and with power and dominion, He charged life to come back. The revealing of Glory breaks the unbelief, hopelessness, and despair of off the minds of people.

The enemy keeps us in our flesh to where we see nothing but the flaws. This is a distraction tactic and will never lead us to productivity or producing fruits of righteousness. You cannot fix yourself or others. Allow God Almighty to perfect His love in you and bring you into the maturity of that love, so you can see the revealed will of God displaying His glory and purpose in you. God strengthens you with the power to walk in His plan and allow yourself to dream and live again (Robin Kirby Gatto). Call forth the destiny lying dormant in the tomb because of the lies you have believed about your identity.

Don't resist the change, embrace and release it. In the fullness of Glory, there is no room for fear. The Glory comes with a high cost. He needs your, "Yes Lord, I'm available." Take steps toward Him. Every step counts. Every meager attempt is a motion of forward progress. You must come to realize that you are having a far greater impact on this side of eternity than you can imagine. Your perception doesn't always reflect the impact that you are having. The price you are paying is far outweighed by the impact God is using you to create. It may feel like you're failing but keep pressing! Even when you stand and hold the line, you are still winning because you aren't backing down. Faint not!

Everything that is a trial in your life serves a greater purpose than you know. Blessed is he who endures trials. God is working so many things together for your greater purpose of His Kingdom. Your hardship will be the platform of your destiny. He is putting all the pieces of the puzzle together. Everything that has happened in your life was preparation for walking in all that God will use you for.

You have a choice to make when you are thrown or forged in the fire. Quitting is not an option if you want to come out a minister of fire. The enemy will attempt to paralyze you with intense pressure from all sides.

For out of the long suffering, perseverance, and steadfastness; endurance will arise. This is where death is defeated. The pressure isn't always from something you're doing wrong. It could be the result of something you're doing right. Stay focused on Christ, not backing down. What you do will determine your outcome. Guard what God has given and entrusted you with. It is very important to stay the course. The enemy tries relentlessly to get you on the run. He wants you to run from destiny, relationships, marriages, churches, etc., so he can get you away from the plans and purposes of God. He knows that he cannot stop you, but he will do everything to delay or abort the plans of God in your life. "I am teaching you to walk by my Spirit," says the Lord. "Not by your circumstances, not by what others say, and not by what the world says. I will direct your path because it is my plan and my timing. "Do not fear." The Holy Spirit will hold firm to God's promises and God's purposes will prevail in your life.

The enemy cannot halt the plans of God. The Holy Spirit has been revealing the areas holding you hostage. Pride and unbelief have kept you from seeing God's truth about your future and His plans for your life. Just remember God works all things for your good. You must keep your focus on Him and not on the past.

The Greek word for flesh is sarkos, speaks to the sinful nature and state of human beings. The sinful nature of the flesh is a power in opposition to the Holy Spirit. The trial is trying to harden, numb, offend, and sadden you. It tries to make you bitter and steal your joy! You must stand firm and resist the enemy. You have to be all in!

We are taught to put it off, but sometimes we lack knowledge in the area we are putting off. Instead we put off the process and God. To be carnally minded is death. Works of the flesh produce death. The mind governed by the flesh is death, but the mind governed by the spirit is life. If this is our spiritual condition, we enter into a dying process as the flesh has brought us here and now that same flesh must die. The opposite of that is the spirit that produces life. His truth will expose every lie you have been believing. Do not hold onto the iniquity of your forefathers. Jesus is the way, the truth, and the life. He is calling your name, saying, "Come! Will you come? Will you cower back in fear and doubt?"

Ephesians 5:8-9, For once you were in darkness, but now you are light in the world. Walk as children of light (for the fruit of the spirit is in all goodness, righteousness, and truth), finding out what is acceptable to the Lord.

Romans 8: 6 -7, for to be Carnally minded is death but to be spiritually minded is life and peace because the carnal mind is that enmity against God For it is not subject to the law of God neither indeed can be.

You can't base where you are going on the place by your present state. You might have to give up some things to get better things. All that opposes you has to do with what God has planned for your future. Get your flesh out of the way and let your circumstances push you closer to destiny. Let them awaken you to God's reality and plan.

You are walking towards a far greater work of glory. Even if it's a little progress, you are still moving in the right direction. Take courage. Step out into all that He has for you. The great unknown where we meet Jesus, where we meet the God of everything.

In 1 Timothy 1:2, Paul said, "Timothy my true son." True sons and daughters will endure the pruning, refining, and cutting away. Beware of the counterfeit that claims you while refusing to go through His processes, which include correction.

He is in the waiting. Why is this taking so long? You will advance through blessing, thankfulness, and hitting your knees. Cry out to the heart of our Father for a sign. We have no clue that God is working it out the whole time. It's a full-circle moment. With the smallest whisper, He ask you to just worship Him to receive His peace. After all the tears of sorrow, you finally shed some tears of joy and rejoicing. He will come through at the midnight hour.

When you are at the end of what you can do, God steps in. He waits for you to give it to Him. I share this with joy in my heart, but also to give hope to all of those who still have the ache in their hearts of unrealized breakthrough. I hope that my testimony gives you the hope in your waiting to keep ahold of the Anchor. God is working it all out even when we cannot see it. Be encouraged that if God can do it for me, He can do it for you.

Through Jesus' precious work, we become unconquerable, immoveable, and we gain resistance to the abrasion of the enemy. We are given an identity seal in our hearts where His values are stored. We gain a position of authority to walk in. We will be a powerful warrior, a soldier for Christ, full of confidence and full of glory. You have been equipped, empowered for spiritual warfare. God has purified you and baptized you with fire. You are armed with the power of God and all of heaven is with you. Rise up and awake, oh sleeper. Be not dismayed or afraid! Be anxious for nothing! We cannot be led by our feelings, emotions, or people. The enemy creates chaos, pain, and suffering. He steals your peace, joy, time, and sleep.

Are you weary, carrying a heavy burden? Come to me. I will refresh your life, for I am your oasis —(Matthew 11:28 TPT).

God sets up (allows) the circumstance so only He can get the glory. You will say, "Only God could do that! Is there anything too hard for God?" Abraham stood on the promises of God when his faith was under siege. He never questioned God. He kept going on His word. We must choose to maintain our position of faith in all circumstances. Our flesh may fail and become weak, but our spirit is strong in Him! He gives us a measure of faith to trust what He says and endure the assignment on our lives. Revelation 5 speaks of the redemptive plan of God, which foreshadowed the inauguration of Jesus Christ and is now being revealed in its victorious consummation (*Ezekiel:2-9, 10, Hebrews 2:5-10*). Christ is our symbol of power and authority. No one else is worthy of executing and revealing God's will and testament in the fullness of time (*Eph. 1:9-10*).

The symbol of the lamb is strength, meekness, and a sacrificial offering. The fact that the lamb was slain but living shows the power with which He overcame. He overcame death and the grave to fulfill God's redemptive plan that was once concealed but now can be revealed and accomplished with complete and perfect power, knowledge, and insight.

That's great news, my friend. The Holy Spirit is at work to redeem sinners. We will sing a new song in response to God's redemptive act in history. God in Christ has inaugurated the church age. The same ascription of praise is accorded to the Lamb as to the Creator. As a royal priesthood, the Saints reign now with Christ on the earth by their worship, prayers, and witness in Word and deed.

This sense of praise is in progress now and throughout redemptive history. Every created being joins the cosmic chorus and ascribes to the lamb every attribute of God. All history is moving toward the predestined goal of the eventual and ultimate universal recognition of the Lordship of Jesus Christ.

We cannot continue to bow at the altar of this world. In the toughest of battles, we forever need reminding of the power that set us free. There is a grace to carry you when your heart is under fire. The cross bears the burden of the one who set you free. From where I was to where I need to be, He is with me. In the darkness, He is with you. The darkness cannot stay where His light abounds. The light shines in the darkness and the darkness can never extinguish it (*John 1:5*).

In our darkness we cannot see what He is doing or where we are going. The more we seek Him, the more we find Him. The more we know Him, the more we will feel His heartbeat. It's in our suffering that we must believe He loves us. Even when it doesn't make sense, we have to let the Holy Spirit lead us in all truth. He will teach you to lean on Him. He strips everything away until all you have is Him. As children of God, we become stuck buried under the weight of shame. Find peace in the desperate place! Have you ever been in a really dark place?

When you feel like you're failing, know you are being held. When you feel so weak, know that He is your strength. Know your God is with you and He is strong. The enemy shouts, "You don't belong!" to keep you feeling unworthy. Stop believing the lie. You are enough. Your identity is found in Him. The enemy doesn't want you to have intimate time with the Lord. Lord, help my unbelief. Let faith arise inspite of all the enemy does to snuff it out. My God is faithful. Every word He spoke is true.

Take all that you have, lay it at His feet, and drink from His cup. Lay back against Him and breathe! See Him and know He is there. He will meet you in your darkest place, so cry out in the deep places of your soul. He will never leave you or forsake you! Nothing can separate you from Him except you.

The unseen realm is constantly moving. Sometimes, we find ourselves stuck because we didn't do the last thing God told us to do. We are lost without Him because we are made to worship and have an intimate relationship with Him. He is enough! Our response to trials and tribulations in our lives reflects our level of trust and faith in God.

It is in Jesus you were taught with regard to your former way of life, to put off your old self which is being corrupted by deceitful desires, to be made known in the attitude of your minds; and to put on the new self, created to be like God in true righteousness and holiness (*Ephesians 4:21-24*).

Celebrate your "yes" to let it all go. Our King is letting go of the residue and hollow things. Let go of the wrong thoughts, pride, and ego. Empty yourself of these things and receive all He has for you. He will fill you up. Celebrate the wonder of His love. Be kind, gentle, and love deeply. Enjoy every day. Receive His grace and mercy because they are new every day. Allow His Spirit to take your spirit where you need to go. Celebrate your wins. Your pit will become your platform. Every day say yes to humility. Humility, meekness, and obedience usher in God's glory! (*Numbers 6:24-25)*, "The Lord bless you and keep you; the Lord make His face to shine upon you."

We can no longer remain silent, sitting on the sidelines, allowing the enemy to restrain and trample us under his feet. He is under our feet. The Lord gave me a dream about this very thing when my heart was under fire. In the dream, I was walking down a street and this unknown man came up to me, yelled, and pointed his finger in my face. "YOU HAVE BEEN GIVEN THE KEYS TO THE KINGDOM NOW USE THEM!" That woke me right up! No explanation is needed. I needed that jolt because I was being lukewarm and complacent. We must be diligent to do our part, bind and loose the demonic realm fighting against us.

Luke 10:19 (AMPC), Behold! I have given you authority and power to trample upon serpents and scorpions and (physical and mental strength and ability) over all power that the enemy possess, and nothing shall in anyway harm you.

Revelation 2:20 (TPT), But I have this against you; You are forgiving that woman Jezebel, who calls herself a prophetess and is seducing my loving servants. She is teaching that it is permissible to indulge in sexual immorality and to eat food sacrificed to idols.

Stop tolerating the enemy.

John 1:12-14 (TPT), But those who embraced Him and took hold of His name, He gave authority to become the children of God! He was not born by the joining of human parents or the natural means, or by a man's desire, but he was born of God. And so, the living expression became a man and lived among us! We gazed upon his Glory, the Glory of the one and only who came from the father overflowing with tender mercy and truth!

You can release it and let it all go! His peace is like a river, you'll just melt in His peace. There is healing power in His presence! Make your life and worship a living altar. Don't withhold anything! It's in your worship and knowing His presence that you will begin to trust Him.

Matthew 11:29-30 (TPT), Simply join your life with mine. Learn my ways and you'll discover that I'm gentle, humble, easy to please. You will find refreshment and rest in me. Vs 30 For all that I require of you will be pleasant and easy to bear.

You are the temple of the Holy Spirit, and you are exactly who God wants to carry His beauty.

You are precisely the right one to display His glory because He purposely hid you for such a time as this.

The struggle will be worth the glory that is coming.

In your unwavering trust, your faith will rise up! Your faith is powerful! It moves the heart of God. When the way becomes blurry, you must adjust your faith to see the dark so you see His perspective, plans and strategies for your situation. In great faith, you will begin to see your giants fall! In His mercy and grace is the fullness of joy! Grace is a gift from God, but will you receive it by faith? Will you open His precious gift? Most people never open the gift and eat the goodness thereof. His grace doesn't leave you the same. Grace doesn't focus on your sin or wait for you to be perfect. To receive grace, we must remain humble. If I humble myself, then grace will lift me up. Because of His amazing love, we Honor Him. I cannot believe the love He has shown. You cannot outrun the love of God. I didn't know what I was missing. I didn't know how much I'd need His presence, His endless mercy and grace.

Jesus loves all of the people most people run from.

I want to remind you of who He is. He is loving, faithful and constant.

He never changes! He is always with you. His love is so deep. It's overwhelming. Did you know He calls you friend? Yield your heart to Him! Intimacy with Jesus opens the heavens, as in (*John 1:51*) (Nathanial's open heaven). The enemy tries to shut down your prayers because he knows your prayers open heaven.

The Holy Spirit comes and rests in this place and teaches us to be one with Him! He alone breaks the hold of darkness. He is high above all darkness bringing freedom and hope. Put your hope and trust in Him alone. He won't disappoint you!

You will find your victory in the presence of the King of Kings! We must become one with Him. He never fails. He has never lost a battle! The battle has already been won. Our Champion is alive. See your victory and worth in Him. Know that you have value as a child of God, from your Heavenly Father, to fulfill your assignment on earth.

Hebrews 6:18-19 (TPT), So it is impossible for God to lie. For we know that His promise and vow will never change! And now we have run into his heart to hide ourselves in his faithfulness. This is where we find his strength and comfort, for he empowers us to seize what has already been established ahead of time- an unshakable hope!

In the Bible, Jesus is the hope of our glory! He is our steadfast stability for eternal life and our lifeline to the Father. He is a strong, trustworthy anchor, firm and secure. He is our lasting hope! We have this certainty and hope like a strong, unbreakable anchor holding our souls to God Himself. We can hold tight to His promises. He promised to never leave us or forsake us.

THE ANCHOR HOLDS

His love is our consistent foundational anchor. That anchor is fastened to the mercy seat which sits in the Heavenly realm beyond the sacred threshold, and where Jesus, our forerunner, has gone before us. Our connection to Him is our only hope in these most uncertain times. Jesus is the anchor of where our hope lies.

Jesus, the Anointed One, is always the same-yesterday, today, and forever. — Hebrews 13:8 TPT

He never changes! When you find yourself in the temptations, trials, and storms of life, no matter what happens, God is in control. The anchor holds us in the stormy seas of life, even tighter when your broken spirit, broken heart, and severed will have left you feeling tattered, weary, and fatigued. We come to Him dead, and He brings us back to life. I have learned the beauty of a resurrected life. The redeeming power of His love.

He is our strength when we are weak. Human weakness is not a liability because it makes room for the power of God. The Bible is full of people who were weak at times. The Lord works in our weakness. Though our flesh may fail, His spirit is strong in us. He gives you the strength and the power to walk in your divine purpose and the destiny He planned for your life. He gives us His perfect peace and strength! Our weakness facilitates dependence on God, which cultivates the appropriation of grace, and ascribes all Glory and credit to God. Therefore, I will gladly boast about my weaknesses so that the power of Christ dwells in me. When we embrace weakness, we have looked at ourselves long enough to know that we cannot make it without looking at another. We realize how badly we need God.

2 Cor. 12:9, but he said to me, my grace is sufficient for you, for my power is made perfect in weakness. Therefore, I will boast all the more gladly about my weaknesses, so that Christ power may rest on me.

Thankfully God does not just leave us there when we abide in Him. He looks at us through the blood-stained eyes of His only begotten Son, seeing a lost and dying world. He died so that we could be brought to life. His blood brings back life. This is your season of breakthrough; this is your time to come forth and rejoice as we overcome by the Blood of the Lamb and the word of our testimony. When God appears to you, it is no mistake. The Holy Spirit is the one who has drawn you in. What will you do with your second chance? You are a chosen one: the remnant. Even when you do not understand where God is taking you, become invested and pursue Him. You will find Him and uncover the hidden treasures and the mystery of His Word and revelation as He relentlessly pursues you.

Just find the strength to carry on. You have been equipped with everything you need to overcome. Never look back! Break ties from the past. You ultimately cannot move or change yourself or anyone else. Only the power of God can. God is more than able to do it. But will you trust Him to do it? Do you believe that God will do it for you? I had so much unbelief that God would do it for me. You must understand our ways are not God's and He has a plan. The Holy Spirit will lead you, but will you follow? Will you do what the Holy Spirit is asking you to do? Sometimes, it is not always what we want or think it should be, but He knows the way.

God's plan may not always make sense to you because His ways are not our ways. You will not be able to follow your own human logic, understand the journey or battlefield you have entered. You must learn to walk in a new level of faith and trust in the Father. As you learn to trust in Him and abide in His Word, new pieces will be added to the puzzle, which will all come together for God's master plan. God can restore what is broken and change it into something amazing. All you need is faith. It is God's desire to change our circumstances and his ability to transform our hearts. God is faithful. He is with you always. He is for you. He hears your cries and your prayers.

He is working it all out for you. He loves you so much, more than you can think, ask, or imagine. He works according to His goodness and power. When you feel less than, like you don't measure up, it's not the Spirit of the living God. When we mature as Christians, we can move past problems in our own lives, look to God, and have hope. We must allow God to work through us to rescue others by overcoming and walking out our testimonies. Your past or present circumstances should not keep you from moving forward. Put your trust in God and let your faith supersede the past while choosing to let go. Consider what God has for your future. Stop looking back. You're not going that way. You cannot see the road ahead while looking back at what is familiar. Sometimes we choose the old road even if it's chaotic and reckless because it's familiar. It takes courage to let go and move into the unknown. You can start to embrace healing once you face what you're letting go of. Your past cannot go with you. You must let it go so the new thing can spring forth.

What opposes you has to do with what God has planned for your future. Some people come into your life for a season. We become emotionally attached to them and do not like it when they go. Sometimes it is a part of God's plan for them to leave. Not everyone will complete the journey with you.

Communion puts us in alignment and unity with the Lord. Our spirit should be over our flesh: your works versus being led by the spirit. Allow the Holy Spirit to lead. Your life will become an altar. It's where you come alive. The altar is a place of restoration and victory. Don't look to man but look to God. Most often, it is a natural behavior to look for approval in your situation. However man's perspective may not be God's and therefore, it could lead you astray.

I am living proof of the mercy and grace of God. He turned my whole life upside down. If you knew me then and seen me now, it's a miracle that I can still give God glory and praise. He took the deadness and brought me back to life, healed and whole. He took the old things and made me new. His sacrifice, goodness, faithfulness, and persistent pursuit is the reason that I have been able to overcome. I'm so thankful my freedom wasn't based on what I deserved because of my sin. I would still be lost and broken. There is power in the cross and the blood of Jesus.

I'm alive to tell the story because the power of my Savior's blood. The cross that He carried was for all eternity.

To surrender is to relinquish your will to His. God is not going to go against your will. He waits for us to ask, release it to Him, and then let it all go. There is no freedom or victory without Him. In that same way, when we are without Christ, we are just sitting at the beautiful gate but can't enter in our own strength. We don't yet have a Christian walk. We need a miracle. We need something beautiful to happen. Your confidence grows in the faithfulness of God. You live by faith, or you live in fear. God increases your faith as you walk out your faith journey. God changes us through His grace. We cannot change ourselves. We must go to God and let Him fight for us. His grace is one-sided. He isn't asking you for anything in return.

It's not too late to come home. It's not too late for God to resurrect the dry bones that lay in waste, or the dormant gifts that still lay in the tomb. There isn't anyone too far gone or too far out that can't be rescued and saved. He is the God of the impossible. He is with you until the very end. Even when you say no, He still sings over you and speaks out your breakthrough. The One who knows you, who called you, who reversed the curse, and then gave light that came flooding in to light up your darkness.

When Heaven and Earth collide, fire falls and miracles happen. Hosea, whose name means salvation or deliverance, was chosen by God to live out His message to God's people by marrying a woman who was unfaithful to him. His sensitivity toward the sinful condition of his countryman and the loving heart of God fitted him for the difficult ministry. The Book of Hosea is about a people who needed to hear the love of God and the unique way God chose to demonstrate His love for His people.

Hosea describes the characteristic social conditions of his day with corrupt leaders, unstable family life, widespread immorality, hatred, and poverty. Though people continued a form of worship, idolatry was more accepted by the priest, who failed to guide the people into ways of righteousness. Despite the darkness of these days, Hosea holds out hope to inspire his people to turn back to God.

The problem was getting this message of God's love to a people who were not inclined to listen and were not likely to understand even if they did listen. God's solution was to let the prophet be his own sermon. Hosea was to demonstrate God's love for Israel through his love for Gomer. *"Go love again (Hosea 3:1)."* If the people around us do not see the love of God in us, then where could they ever find it?. Like Hosea, all believers are called to demonstrate to their neighbors by their attitude and by their actions in God's love in Christ to a world blindly groping for indications of authentic love. The only perfect examples of love are found in God.

When God enters into marriage with His people, He recites vows that promise permanence, a right relationship, fair treatment, love unfailing, tenderness, security, and continuing self-revelation (*Hosea 2:19-20*). Our love must drink from this spring, then draw for others, offering not the best form of human love we can give but the pure, undiluted love of God in Christ.

The Book of Hosea teaches two outstanding lessons concerning the Holy Spirit. First, it is important to depend on the presence of the Holy Spirit. Second, negative things happen when the Holy Spirit is missing from a life. Twice Hosea uses the phrase the spirit of harlotry in (*Hosea 4:12, 4:5*) and speaks of the consequences of being filled with an unholy spirit. Like Paul in Ephesians, Hosea compares an unholy spirit to wine, which enslaves the heart.

The spirit of harlotry can also cause people to remain in false worship. The Holy Spirit guides us in true ways. On the other hand, the spirit of harlotry keeps people from knowing God. The love of Hosea for his wayward wife reminds us of the preeminent fruit of the spirit of love (*Galatians 5:22*). The love of God has been poured out in our hearts through the Holy Spirit, who has been given to us (*Romans 5:5*).

In Galatians, Paul teaches that Jesus places those who have faith in Him in a position of liberty, freeing them from bondages, legalism, and license. Apostles' main emphasis is on the crucifixion of Christ as the basis for the believer's deliverance from the curse of sin, self, and the law. Paul also describes a dynamic faith union with Christ, visibly portrayed in baptism, which relates all believers as brothers and sisters. Paul asked the Galatians who would readily admit that they had begun their Christian life by the spirit. They were seeking spiritual maturity by performing works of the law. The intimation is that the same spirit who regenerated them causes new life to grow. Paul asked a similar question concerning the Holy Spirit. The verb supplies suggest a continual provision in bountiful measure. At the same time, works indicate that God continued to perform miracles in their midst through spirit-filled believers who had not slipped into legalism.

The word "miracles" refers to the Spirit's charismatic manifestation evidenced by outward signs such as those described in (*1 Corinthians 12-14*). The phrase "the promise of the spirit" was also used by Peter to explain the outpouring of the Holy Spirit at Pentecost in (*Acts 2:33*). This verse teaches that we receive the Holy Spirit by faith and that Spirit continues to manage Himself in power as we walk in faith.

Paul graphically describes a fierce and constant conflict between the flesh. Only by the Holy Spirit, when we submit to His control by actively walking in Him, are we able to die of the flesh. We can be delivered from the tyranny of the law, which causes the fruit of holiness to grow in our lives. The calls exportation concerning the proper use of the Christian liberty apart from the controlling sanctifying work of the Holy Spirit liberty is certain to degenerate into license.

In the dream I found myself walking down a street, I sang with a microphone and praised the Lord. I was singing so beautifully, and I remembered thinking, "Wow. I didn't know that I sounded that good." All of a sudden, a wall of weeds, branches, and rock appeared, blocking me from moving any farther. With no hesitation and while still holding on to the microphone with one hand, I grabbed the branches with my other hand and started to climb the wall. I just kept praising and worshiping. I climbed with ease to the top and then over. When I woke up, I said, "Wow. God, is it really that easy when we face huge obstacles to worship, praise, thank you and just climb right up and over with ease?" The Lord used this dream to show me how the importance and power of our worship, praise and thanksgiving. It can literally be the difference between staying stuck and moving ahead with ease. There is nothing more displeasing to the Lord than our murmuring, complaining, and ungratefulness, no matter the circumstances.

God is creating a movement! He is awakening the sleeping soul. The sons and daughters are awakening. Their dead hearts are being brought to life. All creation is groaning and waiting for God's sons and daughters to realize their identity. There is a resurrection power that lives in us and sets us free. God says, "I am giving you prophetic vision into the heavenly realm so you can gain your father's perspective on things to come. Your vision has been dulled. You have been operating without full knowledge and sight. I am bringing you into the divine order of my perfect will. I have called you to wage warfare against the enemy, to stand in a posture of faith. Your warfare and struggle are because of the movement of my Spirit that's coming. You will receive a new wind of strength for the coming battle. You have been wrestling for the revolution and reformation that is coming. The world has been under the influence of a spirit of addiction, death, and destruction. There has been a public display of sin and darkness today. The world has been in a place of idolatry, self-worship, and their fleshy works are filtering in and plaguing my church."

God's people are operating in the flesh and not in the power of His Spirit. He is coming in like a flood of transformation and reformation to the people of the nations. He is raising up the broken to life. The living power of redemption is coming! The hearts of people are cold and spiritually dead. They are crushed and broken in spirit. They are like dead men walking, a slave to their own sin. They are walking aimlessly in the valley of the shadow of death. They have lost their ability to see, which has made the future unclear. Their hope and faith are gone.

They find their souls in a dry and thirsty place, overwhelmed by the darkness all around them. They are pressed and held down by that which opposes them. Fear has gripped the hearts of many, as they are drowning in worldly, fleshy works. I feel that it is part of my calling to make sure people know that they are not left in dark places, feeling forsaken.

The enemy has over-played his hand because it's in our weakness that God's Glory appears. His Glory is coming in like a flood, a mighty sound of Heaven is rushing in. He will be pouring out His Spirit on His sons and daughters. His divine assistance will rescue and deliver the nations. Do you see that He has called you to partner with Heaven and be a deliverer of the generations? He is trusting you with a healing ministry. It is your spiritual inheritance.

He is lifting you up to higher spiritual heights, with new authority, to rule and reign in His strength and protection. The past season has left you feeling the pressure of the intense transformational time that you were in. You are being transformed by the power of His presence. His restoration is coming upon you, giving you the ability to bring restoration to others. In the past, the enemy has shut your mouth and vision so you couldn't see, speak, or prophesy. He tried to take you out before your time. You will declare and decree with great boldness, "You will live and not die."

Your delay has come to meet where the promises of God are, and suddenly a sound like a roaring and violent wind comes down from Heaven and fills the whole house. It's His strong wind that breaks your silence. His Kingdom is coming on the wind of His Spirit and power to blow through and do what only He can do.

He is destroying the stronghold and curse of the spirit of death and setting His people free. This is the era of the mouth, and you will walk in the office as His prophet with great boldness.

He is opening up blind eyes to see clearer. He is opening up the heavens. He is giving you 20/20 vision for the revolution and reformation that is coming in the wind of His revival. As God comes down and meets with you, He reveals what you are to do. He declares, "I am sending you as a revolutionary messenger in battle." You will come together with the Father, Son, and Holy Spirit. You will walk in authority and truth. You will carry God's Glory. You will have a healing anointing. You will be laying hands on the sick and they will recover. You will walk in the authority and power to raise the dead. You will have victory in conflict as His warrior in the revival or harvest of souls blowing in. Can you feel the wind stirring?

I would like to share a dream I was given. My husband and I were on an airplane, looking out the window. I then noticed a ceremonial procession. It was a mass of people coming together and joining in at the base of a mountain. The land was very rich and plush. The procession was very elegant, elaborate, and of royal quality. It was very long and far reaching.

The procession was constantly moving forward, with many activities folding in. I could see a bride walking. The bride was like a giant and encircled by red roses. The roses were so beautiful and grouped in bushels. They were singing and dancing in a circular motion around the bride, in celebration of the bride. The bride was crowned with splendor and glory.

I suddenly realized that I was supposed to be a part of the wedding. I was the maid of honor, and I was running late. My husband was unaware that we were running late. I felt such an urgency to take my rightful place in the procession. The plane landed at a hotel. I was then led to a room where a lady was waiting to help prepare me for my role as maid of honor.

The room was a place of preparation for the bridesmaids to get ready for the wedding. The first thing that I had to do was get undressed. There was a beautiful green dress awaiting me. It was emerald green, a representation of the throne of God. I began to undress in front of a mirror, taking off the old clothes to prepare for my new role in the procession. As I considered the role of maid of honor, I then realized that I was supposed to prepare a speech for the reception, and I had not done that. I was feeling very rushed and unprepared.

I believe that many are lagging and running late because of the enemy's distractions. They are not prepared to walk in the mantel, anointing, and authority that has been given to them by the Father. The church is the bride of Christ. I'm writing this book to help individuals realize their life has a purpose, fully planned by God to usher in His Glory of the end-time battle. The Lord is coming in a fury against the darkness of hell, and we have a part to play in this happening, but we must get prepared and be ready.

The Holy Spirit is training us to reflect and mirror the image of Christ in the earth. Those with the eagle and watchman anointing are being trained to prepare and equip the bride. John the Baptist, a forerunner, pioneer, and trailblazer like says, "I delight to see the bridegroom with the bride."

Someone called to change a generation or a nation: making a way, plowing through with perseverance and steadfastness. That is the spirit of Elijah's anointing. The mantle of Elijah is the office of a prophet. This anointing takes years of training in the making with only the help of the Holy Spirit. The Holy Spirit is your mentor for this mantle.

There is a shout arising on earth of the Elijah calling, those coming in acceleration, greater anointing, and greater vision to confront the Jezebel Spirit. There will be a showdown on the horizon. We must be prepared as the enemy wages a relentless war against our inheritance as children of God. The Lord is handing out assignments and mandates in this hour, looking for those who will harken to the clarion call, being urgently sent out. There have been high-level attacks and activity in the unseen realm. Many are feeling the intense pressure of the darkness being ushered in. Christ and His angels are the defenders of the unseen realm. His angels are assisting and defending us in this life. God will protect the call of God and the anointing on your life.

God promised Moses He would fill the whole earth with His Glory! I had a vision of a waterfall where the water was flowing amazingly fast. The Lord said He would pour out His glory through me like that waterfall.

John 7:38 (CEV), "Have faith in me, and you will have life-giving water flowing from deep inside you."

Philp. 2:12 (NLT), "Work hard to show the results of your salvation. Obeying God with reverence and fear."

About The Author

Alena Moore is a co-founder of Behind The Chair Ministries. Alena is a prophetess, operating in discernment, words of knowledge, prophetic intercession, and healing. She is making a difference in the lives of the broken-hearted. Alena is a passionate freedom fighter instilling hope, faith, love, and peace through the Word of God. She is a light bearer and a carrier of the Glory of God piercing into the darkness, bringing healing, deliverance, and restoration for the wounds in the soul. It's her heart's desire to expose the enemy's lies that keep the Body of Christ held captive through unforgiveness, bitterness, anger, and offense. Unforgiveness is plaguing believers and unbelievers alike. It is the Father's heart to set His people free from all that oppresses them—imparting inner healing and deliverance ministry bringing restoration for the Children of God back to the Father, who is our life source. Alena is a hairdresser. Behind

The Chair Ministries was birthed with her friend Carlen during their time working in the hair salon. Alena resides in Missouri with her husband Kevin of 31 years. The couple have four children: Jennifer, Jacob (Heather), Ashlee, Kevin 2nd (Hannah), and seven grandchildren: Connor, Collin, Mason, Elliana, Kevin 3rd, Kason, and Lucas.

References

1. "Satan." Wikipedia. Wikimedia Foundation, May 3, 2022. https://en.wikipedia.org/wiki/Satan.

2. Schatzline, Pat, and Karen Schatzline. Rebuilding the Altar: A Bold Call for a Fresh Encounter with God. Lake Mary, FL: Charisma House, 2017, p. 119, paragraph 1.

3. Verrett, Bethany. "Understanding the Spiritual Gift of Discernment." biblestudytools.com. Salem Web Network, November 15, 2020. https://www.biblestudytools.com/bible-study/topical-studies/understanding-the-spiritual-gift-of-discernment.html.

4. www.dictionary.com. 2022. Definition of withstand | Dictionary.com. [online] Available at: <https://www.dictionary.com/browse/withstand> [Accessed 20 March 2022].

5. "Plumb-Line- Are You All Measured up for God? – Amos 7." Biblical Thoughts, April 19, 2015. https://talkativeangel.wordpress.com/2014/07/08/plumb-line-are-you-all-measured-up-for-god-amos-7/.

6. "Downloads – Kanaan Ministries." Accessed May 11, 2022. https://www.kanaanministries.org/downloads/.

7. Britannica, T. Editors of Encyclopaedia. "Jezebel." Encyclopedia Britannica, January 6, 2021. https://www.britannica.com/biography/Jezebel-queen-of-Israel

8. Omartian, S., 2002. The power of a praying nation. Eugene, Or.: Harvest House, p. 22, paragraph 2.

9. www.dictionary.com. 2022. Definition of repentance | Dictionary.com. [online] Available at: <https://www.dictionary.com/browse/repentance> [Accessed 20 March 2022].

10. Skones, S., Skones, S. and Skones, S., 2022. A Life of Repentance? — Living Word Fellowship. [online] Living Word Fellowship. Available at: <https://www.livingwf.org/news/2019/8/25/a-life-of-repentance> [Accessed 20 March 2022].

11. 2022. [online] Available at: <https://biblehub.com/topical/p/perdition.html.> [Accessed 20 March 2022].

12. BibleProject. 2022. Covenants: The Backbone of the Bible | BibleProject™. [online] Available at: <Https://Bibleproject.com/Blog/Covenants-The-Backbone-Bible> [Accessed 20 March 2022].

13. biblestudytools.com. 2022. Salvation - Biblical Meaning and Definition in Christianity. [online] Available at: <https://www.biblestudytools.com/dictionary/salvation/> [Accessed 20 March 2022].

14. Buttner, Len. "Post Author:Len Buttner." Eagle Ascend. Accessed May 11, 2022. https://eagleascend.com/distinctive-kinds-of-prophetic-utterances/.

15. En.wikipedia.org. 2022. Glory (religion) - Wikipedia. [online] Available at: <https://en.wikipedia.org/wiki/Glory_(religion)> [Accessed 20 March 2022].

16. Price, P., 2006. The prophet's dictionary. New Kensington, Pa.: Whitaker House.

17. "Slain In The Spirit." Wikipedia. Wikimedia Foundation, February 2, 2022. https://en.wikipedia.org/wiki/Slain_in_the_Spirit

18. Francis Brown, Samuel Rolles Driver, and Charles Augustus Briggs, Enhanced Brown-Driver-Briggs Hebrew and English Lexicon (Oxford: Clarendon Press, 1977), 458. For the word "glory" from Exodus 33:18.

19. Life, Hope & Truth. 2022. Chris Moen. [online] Available at: <https://lifehopeandtruth.com/authors/chris-moen/> [Accessed 20 March 2022].

20. Price, P., 2006. The prophet's dictionary. New Kensington, Pa.: Whitaker House, pg. 189, 432

21. 1988. Life application Bible. Wheaton, Ill.: Tyndale House.

22. https://www.biblegateway.com/resources/encyclopedia-of-the-bible/Forgiveness

23. Bultmann, Rudolf, and Robert Morgan. Theology of the New Testament. Waco, TX: Baylor University Press, 2007.

24. "Pattern - Definition, Meaning & Synonyms." Vocabulary.com. Accessed March 20, 2022. https://www.vocabulary.com/dictionary/pattern.

25. "Cycle - Definition, Meaning & Synonyms." Vocabulary.com. Accessed March 20, 2022. https://www.vocabulary.com/dictionary/cycle

26. GotQuestions.org. "Home." GotQuestions.org, August 27, 2015. https://www.gotquestions.org/gift-discerning-spirits.html.

27. Fran O'Donnell says, "Evil Forebodings," A New Thing Ministries, March 26, 2020, https://anewthingministries.com/evil-forebodings/.

28. Lipscomb, Pamela. "What Is a Spiritual Soul Tie?" Spiritual Gifts Today, June 13, 2017. https://spiritualgiftstoday.com/what-is-a-soul-tie/.

29. Evans, Richard Paul. The Road Home. Waterville, ME: Thorndike Press, a part of Gale, a Cengage Company, 2020.

30. Chery, F., 2022. 22 Important Bible Verses About Come As You Are. [online] Bible Reasons | Bible Verses About

Various Topics. Available at: <https://biblereasons.com/come-as-you-are/> [Accessed 20 March 2022].

31. https://www.cslewis.org/blog/a-word-of-grace-march-14-2011

32. Celine. "Difference between Kavod and Shekina." Difference Between Similar Terms and Objects, August 15, 2013. http://www.differencebetween.net/miscellaneous/culture-miscellaneous/difference-between-kavod-and-shekina/.

Index

A

G

I

L

M

R

S

U

unbelief, 58, 67, 123, 124, 171, 172, 178, 182, 186, 190, 208, 220, 225, 253, 254, 257, 262, 264, 269, 276
Unbelief, 123
unbelievers, 15, 177, 227, 289
unclean spirit, 2
unforgiveness, 31, 76, 97, 142, 143, 144, 160, 161, 181, 185, 199, 200, 220, 242, 289
union, 48, 119, 281
unity, 106, 277
universe, 70
unlovable, 161, 173, 203, 212
unneeded, 172
unrighteousness, 48, 50, 114
unsuccessful, 172
unwanted, 172, 212, 217
unworthy, 32, 51, 78, 131, 133, 172, 214, 224, 269

V

Vacation Bible School, 29
vanity, 187
veil, 52, 160, 178
vessel, 25, 33, 63, 77, 236
victim, 10, 33, 39, 88, 137, 169, 172, 194, 200, 205, 208, 209, 212, 213, 214, 217, 220, 244, 250
victory, 5, 10, 37, 38, 50, 56, 75, 116, 124, 125, 126, 127, 148, 149, 183, 184, 185, 236, 247, 253, 258, 273, 278, 285
violence, 31

Y

Z

www.ingramcontent.com/pod-product-compliance
Lightning Source LLC
Chambersburg PA
CBHW070904120626
46546CB00001B/136